OUR DAYS ARE NUMBERED

Getting Ready for Eternity

OUR DAYS ARE NUMBERED

Getting Ready for Eternity

Georges Chevrot

Scepter

Where indicated, some passages in this work have been translated by the publisher for the purposes of this publication.

Certain quotations may have been stylistically adjusted to ensure consistency throughout the text.

This English translation is published with permission from Jean Chevrot, Paris, France.

Published by Scepter Publishers, Inc.
info@scepterpublishers.org
www.scepterpublishers.org
800-322-8773
New York

Cover Image: Courtesy pixabay.com

Cover Design: Rose Design Publishing and Illustration
Text Design and Pagination: Rose Design Publishing and Illustration

Paperback ISBN: 978-1-59417-550-3
Ebook ISBN: 978-1-59417-551-0

Library of Congress Control Number: 2025930106

Printed in the United States of America

Contents

Introduction

Parousia

A little-noticed word shows up in the Gospels toward the end of the liturgical year. In the final Sundays before Advent, the Church directs our piety with a repeated insistence on the expectation of the "Parousia." This Greek word means presence and arrival, with specific reference to the Second Coming of Our Lord Jesus Christ, who will return to judge the living and the dead, and begin the glorious phase of the kingdom of God. The first Christian generation awaited the Lord's return as if it were a forthcoming event. These first followers liked to repeat a brief declaration that expressed their fervent desires: "Maran-atha," or "Come, O Lord!"

Christians long believed that the Parousia would take place at an unknown date, which could still be a long way off. Yet they considered it their duty to prepare themselves and the world for Christ's Second Coming. Traces of this fixation on the Second Coming appear in many Masses, but it is undoubtably the main theme of the final weeks of the liturgical year. If the Parousia and the hope of the Lord's Last Coming holds such a place in the liturgy, it is primarily in answer to the Savior's express command: "Watch therefore, for you know neither the day nor the hour" (Mt 25:13).

The Triumph of Jesus Christ

Today, too many Christians have all but forgotten the need to prepare for Christ's return. They have narrowed their horizons to concern themselves only with their individual salvation, over which most feel a sense of dread. Yet our predecessors in the faith rejoiced above all at the thought of their meeting with the Lord, in which they imagined the dazzling triumph of Jesus Christ.

When Christians take Christ's return seriously, this thought provokes an uncompromising purity of conscience, a stronger faith, and a sustained effort to conquer the world for him when he returns. Their spirits are held in breathless anticipation of this new world. Jesus's resurrection has laid its foundations, and it will finish its construction in the general resurrection. Seen in this way, the hour when each of us bids farewell to this earth is stripped of the sadness that clouds our earthly sojourn. On the contrary, we look forward to death as the dawn of the Parousia. As soon as our hope is habitually turned toward the triumphant Coming of Jesus Christ, we prepare at the same time for the world's salvation and our own.

1

Meeting the Lord: The Second Coming

That you may be blameless on the day of Our Lord Jesus Christ.

—1 Corinthians 1:8

St. Paul summarizes in the above words why believers must prepare for the Second Coming. They took him literally. The first disciples lived in the constant hope that the ascended Lord would soon return to found the new world that would be the definitive kingdom of God. His return would presumably take place "at midnight" (Mt 25:6) preceding the first day of the week. On this sacred day Jesus rose from the dead, and the Holy Spirit was poured out on his Church.

Was it not necessary, following the recommendation of the parable (Lk 12:35), that at the hour of return, he should find them gathered (this is the meaning of the word *ecclesia*), waiting for him, ready to follow him? "Blessed are those servants whom the master finds awake when he comes" (Lk 12:37).

This hope inspired the first organization of Christian worship. Every Saturday evening, when the sabbatical rest was over, the faithful would gather for a prayer vigil, during which they prepared for the long-awaited day of the Parousia, the "Day of the Lord." At vigil's end, they renewed the Lord's Supper, which is both a memorial and an anticipation. Every time Christians renew this meal, as St. Paul writes, they "proclaim the Lord's death (memorial) until he comes (expectation)" (1 Cor 11:26). The Eucharist links Jesus's redemptive sacrifice to his return. The Savior's sacrifice was completed by his resurrection, and the present-day Mass is the pledge of the Christian's own resurrection: It helps them await Christ's return. This doctrine has not changed. Even today, our Mass is like a veiled Parousia, and our Sunday is still the Lord's Day, *dies dominica*, the day when we gather to remember the Lord Jesus and await his return.

The Savior will judge the world on the day when he manifests himself in his glory. The expression "Day of the Lord" thus becomes synonymous with judgment in St. Paul's language, to the point that he sometimes uses the word "day" to designate a human tribunal.[1] The Second Coming, however, brings with it the judgment

1. See 1 Corinthians 4:3 in *Biblia Sacra Vulgata*: "Mihi autem pro minimo est ut a vobis judicer, aut ab humano die: sed neque meipsum judico."

of judgments, far more consequential than any earthly condemnation.

The Apostle therefore reminded his first converts that when they appear before the Lord's tribunal no serious accusation should weigh upon them: "that you may be blameless on the day of Our Lord" (1 Cor 1:8). To be fully exonerated, serious work remains. Paul not only praises but also chastises the young Church at Corinth. Let them not lose heart, however, for Christians have received all the necessary help from God. The Lord Jesus himself will strengthen us, so that at life's end we will not incur his condemnation.

St. Paul also warns us against presumption and despair. If we have the courage to purify ourselves now, it will spare us terror on the last day. Certainly, when we think that our eternity depends on the moment when we meet the Lord, we cannot but feel a sense of dread at first. We repeat with the psalmist: "If thou, O Lord, shouldst mark iniquities, Lord, who could stand?" (Ps 130:3).

Troubled by the memory of sins, we are no less apprehensive of our countless infidelities to grace. Our good Master expected a holiness from us that would have extended his reign over the earth. What negligent servants we will have been—reluctant to do our work, botching our work, always thinking that we have done enough for him! Lastly, and this confounds us to no end, we will never be able to fittingly atone for our faults or make up for the lost time and graces rejected.

Fortunately, the Apostle draws us away from discouragement by turning us from an exclusive consideration of ourselves: “Consequently he is able for all time to save those who draw near to God through him, since he always lives to make intercession for them” (Heb 7:25). Tomorrow he will be our judge. Today he is our advocate with the Father. He is still our Savior.

The faults that will earn us the judge’s punishment later, he now brings before us with all the affection of an elder brother. “Come to me,” he says, “all who labor and are heavy laden, and I will give you rest” (Mt 11:28). We have no friend dearer, more helpful, or more powerful than Christ who will judge us.

2

Forgiveness of Sins: The Paralytic of Capernaum

Take heart, my son; your sins are forgiven.

—Matthew 9:2

In the early days of Jesus's preaching, the Pharisees had not yet openly declared their hostility to Jesus and his fame was attracting enthusiastic crowds. His house in Capernaum had been invaded by visitors: "There was no longer room for them, not even about the door" (Mk 2:2).

A paralytic was carried by four men from his bed, but they were unable to make their way through the crowd blocking the entrance to the house. They quickly made a decision. They climbed the outside staircase leading to the terrace that served as a roof. The roofs of Galilean houses were made of wooden crossbeams supporting reed wainscot covered with clay or packed earth. It was easy for the porters to lift the layer of earth and push aside the reeds. Then, through the opening, they let down the paralytic to Jesus.

Imagine the crowd's astonishment inside the house as they saw the cripple descend in a cloud of dust and stones. But what moves Jesus is the tenacious confidence of the paralytic's friends, who have not shied away from any difficulty to help him. "And when he saw their faith he said to the cripple, 'Man, your sins are forgiven you'" (Lk 5:20).

Going Beyond Illusions

At first sight, the Savior's declaration must have seemed irrelevant. It wasn't what the little group had expected. They had gone to all this trouble for the miracle worker to heal the paralytic. But Jesus didn't seem to pay any attention to the sick man's inert limbs. He looks beyond the infirmities of the body and asserts that there is a more serious evil than physical pain: sin.

The unfortunate man was likely confused about the connection between his infirmity and his sins. A common view among the Savior's contemporaries was that sickness was the punishment for personal or hereditary sins (Jn 9:2). Perhaps he feared that his past faults had made his illness incurable. This would explain the expression that St. Matthew puts on Jesus's lips: "Take heart, my son; your sins are forgiven" (Mt 9:2). In any case, the Lord was eager to convince those he was instructing that sin is the greatest of evils.

We have difficulty hearing this language. Often, we claim the right to choose the conditions of our own happiness, what is right and what is wrong. But this claim to decide good and evil as we please is a usurpation of God's plan. We are part of a universe whose harmony is governed by the laws of the Creator. Human life on earth can only be sustained if it respects the conditions established by the author of life. To go against God's plan is to raise our will above his. We introduce disorder into the world and consequently suffering. Above all, this usurpation creates a definitive rupture between God and ourselves. Sin is folly because divine laws have only man's happiness in mind. Today, we see a world organized outside God's laws, with inhuman results. A sinful world is a world out of alignment, like a planet out of its orbit and orbiting on itself, pursuing a disorderly course through space. It causes untold destruction, until it destroys itself. In fact, St. Paul affirms that the physical universe has suffered the repercussions of man's sin (Rom 8:20).

A Corrupted World

Let's try to understand what it was like for the Son of God to find himself in a disorganized world, totally different from the one that emerged from the Creator's mind. Let's imagine the pain he felt at living in a humanity subject to Satan's influence (1 Jn 5:19). What an affront to his Father! What misfortune for us! Whether Jesus turns to God or looks down on humanity, his heart is equally crushed with pain. He never ceases to see the horrible stain of sin on creation that dishonors God and causes man's misery. Yet Jesus "takes away the sin of the world" (Jn 1:29).

In the house in Capernaum, the sick man lying at his feet may be personally less guilty than many others. He is nonetheless, like every man, like you and me, part of a rebellious humanity. It is the rebellious and condemned human race that Jesus contemplates stretched out on the paralytic's couch. And so he makes known the main object of his mission: "Your sins are forgiven you" (Lk 5:20). Of all the evils that afflict us, sin is the first, and not only our own, but "the sin of the world" which we share. When we know that sin is our undoing, we recognize our need for a savior. Jesus reveals the evil of sin only because he wants to deliver us from it.

Only Jesus knew the reality of sin's malice and evil, and only he could atone for it with his sufferings and annul it with his death. He came for this hour (Jn 12:27), that hour which will avenge his Father's honor and recreate us in a state of holiness. But he did not wait for that hour to announce to man his deliverance: "Man, your sins are forgiven you" (Lk 5:20).

The paralytic from Capernaum wonders if he has heard correctly. The lawyers who witnessed the scene take offense at having understood. They think: *This man (Jesus) blasphemes. He claims divine power since God alone can forgive us our trespasses. When the Messiah comes, he will separate the righteous from the sinners, nothing more.* Jesus reads their minds before they dare express their thoughts. The Messiah will do more than they suppose, for he will be greater than they expect. "Why do you question in your hearts?" he asks the scribes; "The Son of man [Jesus uses the title of judge announced by Daniel] has authority on earth to forgive sins" (Lk 5:22–24). That's easy to say! Easier, no doubt, than giving a cripple the use of his legs.

Proof of Divine Power to Forgive

To prove that the Son of God possesses the divine power of forgiveness, Jesus actually exercises it. "He said to the man who was paralyzed—'I say to you, rise, take up your bed and go home.' And immediately he rose before them, and took up that on which he lay, and went home, glorifying God" (Lk 5:24–25). St. Luke specifies that the man now absolved and healed gave glory to God. These last words teach us to always ask the Lord for forgiveness. We beg his help when temptation arises; but do we thank God for forgiving our sins?

The forgiveness Jesus earned on the cross, he entrusted to the ministers of his Church, who dispense it to sinners. But we have so often received, either in the absolution that precedes communion, or in auricular confession, the assurance of forgiveness that it too rarely produces in us the shock that it should. Doesn't a pardon so easily obtained run the risk of dulling consciences?

We usually think of ourselves first in confession. We want the peace that priestly absolution gives, the courage we obtain after confessing, a lessening of the penalty for our faults, and, to put it bluntly, the joy of forgetting that we have sinned. But in this joy lies a grave danger: that of forgetting we are sinners.

If we have God in view, however, we won't forget that we are forgiven sinners. We will thank God every day for having forgiven us. How many times have we had to repeat the same confession, and God has never wished to doubt our repentance! How many times we would have repeated our faults had he not protected us! "I confess" wrote St. Augustine, "that everything has been forgiven, both the evil things I did of my own accord, and those which I did not do because of your guidance."[1]

---

1. Augustine, *Confessions* 2.15, trans. Henry Chadwick (Oxford University Press, 2009).

"Holiness," remarks Father Frederick Faber, "has lost its principle of growth if it is separated from abiding sorrow for sin. For the principle of growth is not love only, but forgiven love."[2] As Our Lord taught in the parable of the two debtors: "He who is forgiven little, loves little" (Lk 7:47). By keeping alive the memory of God's forgiveness, we become more vigilant, generous, and humble. Our hope rests solely in the one who says: "My son, your sins are forgiven" (Mk 2:5).

---

2. Frederick W. Faber, *Growth in Holiness; or, The Progress of the Spiritual Life* (London: 1855), p. 286.

3

Call of Sinners: Saint Matthew

I came not to call the righteous, but sinners.

—Matthew 9:13

The story of St. Matthew begins in front of a table stacked with coins. It ends at the foot of another table, the Eucharistic table, where he was put to death while celebrating Mass. The former tax collector mingled his blood with that of the Holy Sacrifice and gave Christ the supreme proof of his love. The publican Levi became St. Matthew, apostle and evangelist, because he knew how to hear the two words Jesus spoke to him: "Follow me" (Mt 9:9).

This strange adventure caused quite a stir on the shores of Lake Tiberias. Understandably so. Imagine the scene today, in a provincial town, at the door of the tax collector's office. Some have come to pay their taxes; others have been called in to clear themselves for having paid too little. Both agree that the amount of their contributions is too high. The people are becoming impatient. Why doesn't this usually punctual civil servant open his office? Enquiries are made, and it appears the tax collector left town that morning. He is on his way to the missions to preach Jesus Christ to the tribes of Africa. One can only imagine the commotion this news would have caused. Jesus looked at Levi, who was sitting at the customs office, and said to him, "'Follow me.' And he left everything and rose and followed him." (Lk 5:27–28). The tax collector responds to Jesus's call *instantly, completely, and joyfully.*

Capernaum, a frontier town and busy transit point, had an important customs office. According to the Greek text, Levi was merely a "collector," responsible for collecting taxes under the orders of a chief publican (as was Zacchaeus). His profession was universally reviled. Public treasury officials, the publicans, acted on behalf of the Romans, the dreaded and hated occupiers. This was bad enough. Worse, they added on legal fees for their own benefit. Yet it was one of these men that Jesus invited to follow him. Jesus implicitly condemns the unjust and absurd malice that belittles people on "the other side," as if there couldn't be honest and virtuous people among them. Levi was such a belittled man, and the Master had discerned the quality of his soul. For his part, Levi had already heard of Jesus. No other explanation warrants his quick decision. During his stay in the city, the Savior had performed miracles and preached at length. Perhaps Levi had had the opportunity to listen to him. He felt attracted by his word, but he, a reprobate, would not have dared to appear before the prophet. As always, Jesus takes the lead. No useless speeches, just two direct words: "Follow me." Matthew is immediately won over.

At the Savior's call, Levi got up *right away.* In truth, isn't this the only way to respond to God? When, in response to the promptings of conscience or the inspirations of grace, we say *just now*, we generally let the hour pass. When we say *later*, the will hesitates and steps back: It's too late. Levi doesn't know exactly where his new lord will lead him; but for the moment, he doesn't need to know.

Giving Up Job Security

The Lord asks Matthew for an act of faith. It is necessary for him to perform an act of total renunciation. His job guaranteed him a wage for the next day; now he commits himself to complete insecurity. Following in Jesus's footsteps, he set out on the great adventure of making the earth the kingdom of God. The future apostle doesn't bargain for his help, he doesn't question the one who suddenly tears him away from a normal existence. He gives up everything, knowing nothing of what lies ahead.

Jesus demands total self-giving from all his disciples, because those who give themselves halfway are not giving themselves at all. To give oneself, one must hold nothing back. In his Gospel, St. Matthew is careful not to emphasize the generosity of his gift. St. Luke, who was not bound to the same discretion, tells us: "He left everything, [his office, his house, his country, his family], and rose and followed him" (Lk 5:28). The first four apostles abandoned their nets but did not destroy them (they will take them up again between Easter and Pentecost). The publican has no such resource. In the event of Jesus's enterprise failing, he would be out of work. His past is definitively dead. But now that he has given everything, he is free. He sacrifices even his own name. The other two evangelists tell us that his name was Levi. He calls himself by his new name now, which Jesus no doubt imposed on him as he did on Simon Peter. From then on, he was called Matthew, which means "gift of Yahweh." Nevertheless, he never forgot his origins, nor the Savior's mercy in seeking him out at his tax collector's tent, for, in the list of apostles, he is the only one to add to Matthew's name the formerly infamous epithet, "the tax collector" (Mt 10:3).

A Joyful Acceptance of God's Will

Matthew doesn't flee from the objects he renounces, for fear of being recaptured by their allure. His heart doesn't clench, but, on the contrary, overflows with joy, and Christ's new disciple organizes a banquet to honor his new master. St. Luke tells us: "And Levi made him a great feast in his house" (Lk 5:29). The day he gave up everything to follow Jesus was a day of celebration. Why should he watch his spending, since money no longer had any value in his eyes? He invites all the publicans in the district, all his colleagues in the tax, registration, and customs departments, and others too. In his Gospel, Matthew doesn't hide their character: They were miscreants, "sinners." St. Mark insists there were "many . . . sinners" (Mt 9:10; Mk 2:15).

Jesus presides easily over all these people who had never set foot in the synagogue, and he brought his disciples with him. This is his opportunity to reveal God's mysterious regard for human weakness. In fact, the meal was sure to scandalize the right-thinking local people. Already shocked by Levi's call, the Pharisees and scribes can no longer contain themselves when they see these ne'er-do-wells heading for the publican's house. They take Jesus's disciples to task: "Why does your teacher eat with tax collectors and sinners?" (Mt 9:11). What kind of company is this for a man who claims to be the Messiah! Does he intend to save the world with these sinners? Such prejudices are so tenacious that almost twenty years after Jesus's resurrection, Judaizing Christians in Antioch refuse to eat with "brothers" who had converted from paganism (Gal 2:12).

Jesus is quick to respond to the protests: "Those who are well have no need of a physician, but those who are sick" he tells them (Mt 9:12). Then he advises his detractors to ponder the message of the prophet Hosea: "Go and learn what this means, 'I desire mercy, and not sacrifice'" (Mt 9:13). Because the Pharisees meticulously observed ritual prescriptions, they believed themselves entitled to scorn those who did not.

Those who claim to be impeccable, the so-called righteous, will never understand that Jesus comes to save the unfortunate, who know both guilt and the feeling of weakness. He will found his Church with converted sinners, and with them he will save the world. As for heaven, the kingdom of eternal justice, with the exception of the Blessed Virgin Mary it is filled entirely with sinners. This is why our Savior leans toward those who have failed, to lift them up, and he abandons to presumption those who find no fault in themselves. He calls only sinners. In fact, he came to call everyone! Let us only know that we are all sinners, and he will justify us as soon as we respond to his call.

All Are Called

To all Christians, Jesus repeats the two words that inspired St. Matthew's courageous resolution: "Follow me." All are "called." It would be a mistake to reserve the word "vocation" for certain exceptional states of life. There is only one Christian vocation, albeit with different paths. All Christians are called to share God's glory; all are called to practice the charity that leads to heaven; all are called to perfection. This command obliges us all to "be perfect" (Mt 5:48). Perfection is compatible with all states of life: It is not the privilege of the monastery, nor does it require us to withdraw from ordinary life. Such a restriction would be tantamount to denying the sanctifying value of the Gospel for many people. All Christians, though living in different conditions, are called to follow Jesus and continue his work where Providence has placed them and, when the time has come to choose their path, in the kind of life they have freely chosen.

Following Jesus means believing in him, loving him, imitating him, and obeying him. To all Christians, whoever they may be, God has given the grace to follow his Son. But let's not delude ourselves that we can follow Jesus by standing still. The word is an image: To follow, we must always be walking, always moving forward. The law is the same for everyone: the monk, the priest, the layman; the adolescent, the adult, the old man. No one is allowed to stop. Jesus's first call echoes at every hour of our lives. We don't answer it once and for all on the day of confirmation, or when we enter holy orders, or when we receive the marriage blessing. Every day, as Christians, you must respond in detail to Christ's call: in church, at home, on the street, at your desk.

Reflect upon your own life. Are you sure you have answered all Christ's calls? Beware of being too quick to call yourself "righteous," for it is sinners whom our beloved Master has come to call. Be even more precise: For a long time perhaps, Jesus has been asking you for an effort, a renunciation, or a new advance that you have not yet granted him. It may be that what he expects from you today is small, and yet you hesitate to do it. Offer that little thing to him during the Mass. When you meet the Lord in Communion offer him what he asks of you: immediately, fully, and joyfully.

Especially with joy. When the publican invited his colleagues, he was so happy to be following Jesus that he wanted them to share in his happiness. This joy, which he naively shared with them, was the first testimony he gave to his Master. It was the beginning of his apostolate. Let's face it, the most persuasive apostolate is Christian joy, the joyful serenity that makes others want to be like the Christians they know. But a Christian cannot be happy if he denies something to Jesus Christ. Grant God what he desires, and your joy will draw your companions to him as well. Following St. Matthew's example, you too will become a witness and preacher of the Gospel.

4

The Virtue of Faith: The Wedding Feast

> Friend, how did you get in here without a wedding garment?
>
> —Matthew 22:12

In the parable of the wedding garment, a king invites the city notables to his son's wedding feast. It was only natural that they should all accept the royal invitation and come in full ceremonial dress. All, in fact, were dressed for the occasion—the wedding garment—except one. One man came to the feast in everyday clothes. As the king entered the glittering hall, he caught sight of this man. He said to him, "Friend, how did you get in here without a wedding garment?" But the man remained tight-lipped. He didn't even stammer an excuse; he couldn't find one. Then the king said to the attendants: "Bind him hand and foot, and cast him into the outer darkness; there men will weep and gnash their teeth" (Mt 22:12–13).

The phrase "weeping and gnashing of teeth" is used six times by Matthew. With the exception of a passage in St. Luke (13:28), it is not found in the other evangelists. It is an image of Jewish theology, familiar only to Palestinian readers: After death, the righteous enter the light of God, while sinners, banished from this luminous region, mourn in darkness. The weeping represents their pain, the gnashing of teeth, their anger and despair. This is the supreme punishment. The guest without the garment must have committed a particularly serious offense. What was it?

The wedding garment could refer to the baptismal privileges lost by the Christian who voluntarily rejects the state of grace. The guilty party who cuts himself off from Christ is represented by the guest who refuses to sit at the royal table. Our guest, on the contrary, comes to the feast certain of admission. The parable emphasizes his surprise. He did not expect to be cast out. Our Lord warns us against an illusion that we would deplore at the end of our lives. The Master's lesson is addressed to Christians who believe themselves to be faithful because they come to celebrate the Eucharistic meal every Sunday.

Let's take a closer look. Sensitive to the honor bestowed upon him, even flattered by the prestige that was his due, the careless guest did not refuse the king's invitation and went out of his way to come. But he came as he was; he made no expense for his host;

he paid no heed to his dignity; and he failed to recognize the favor he had received. His sovereign treated him royally. That it was his duty to honor his leader in return never crossed this selfish man's mind. If all he had to do was come and take, he'd be there. As for giving something himself, putting on the wedding garment, he didn't give it a thought. He didn't even realize it was inappropriate.

This is the lesson of the parable. God treats us divinely. He gives the Gospel to us, and he invites us to the Eucharistic meal. In truth, he treats us as only a God can and knows how to do. But do we treat him as we should treat a God? Aren't there Christians who show him less kindness than they show their friends, nor the same attention they pay to those who serve their earthly interests? Do we go out of our way to honor him, obey him, and please him?

Exclusion From Heaven

Our Lord warns us that when the worship of self replaces the worship of God, it leads straight to exclusion from heaven. Religion is above all the worship of God. I'm mistaken if my desires for heaven are absorbed in my own happiness. As if I had a right to it! My salvation is not me, it's the Lord. What we must appreciate in heaven, before our own happiness, is God's incomprehensible love for us and the possibility of knowing him as he knows us and loving him as he loves us. Heaven will be the realization of our present desire to love God. The Lord will be our salvation if we keep the first commandment: "You shall love the Lord your God with all your heart, and with all your soul, and with all your mind, and with all your strength" (Mk 12:30).

And we would also be mistaken to neglect the second commandment, which is similar to the first: "You shall love your neighbor as yourself" (Mk 12:31). Selfish religion degrades salvation into a miserable free-for-all: *As long as I'm OK, I'm not interested in the rest.* The rest, which is the salvation of God's people! The rest, which is the royalty of God acknowledged by redeemed humanity! On the day of the Parousia, the disciple of Christ will only be saved if he has loved his brothers and sisters. No salvation for me, if I have willfully failed to relieve one of the least among Jesus's brothers who were starving, without clothes, or without shelter. No salvation for me if I did not help others to save themselves, if I did not go to the crossroads and along the hedges to gather up the poor, weak, sick, and the blind, and lead them to the threshold of the banqueting hall. Pay attention to the psalm: "Thou hast commanded thy precepts to be kept diligently. O that my ways may be steadfast in keeping thy statutes!" (Ps 119:4-5).

And I'm still wrong if, haggling over my obedience, I only reluctantly give the bare minimum to be saved at the right price. We must always be content with God. We must be content to offer him everything he asks of us, suffering only because we cannot give him more. We must come to him in the wedding garment. This wedding dress is love, and love grows in proportion as egoism diminishes. Preaching on this passage from the Gospel, St. Augustine says to his listeners: "Now you are already inside (the church), you have already come in to the (Eucharistic) banquet, and you are still not wearing a garment in honor of the bridegroom. You are still seeking your own advantage, not that of Jesus Christ."[1]

Let's meditate calmly on these words. If in the practice of religion, I seek only myself, then I am on the wrong track, for in the end I shall find only myself. On the contrary, if we lose sight of ourselves and seek only Jesus Christ, we will find him, and he will save us. If in our prayer we think only of him, he will think of us. If we renounce our will to obey his commandments, he will give us a hundredfold in happiness for what we have sacrificed.

---

1. Augustine, *Sermons 51–94 on the New Testament*, in *The Works of Saint Augustine: A Translation for the 21st Century*, vol. 3, trans. Edmund Hill, ed. John E. Rotelle (New City Press, 1991), p. 451.

The Impulse of Grace

Our Lord is both our helper and our model. He makes us children of God and teaches us to behave like children of God. His Spirit gives us a powerful desire for good, and under his impulse we will grow in virtue and live as new men. Baptism inserts us into the body of Jesus Christ. But baptism is only the beginning. Through the Eucharist, the life of Christ grows within us. We are only baptized *for* the Eucharist, which maintains our union with God and increases Christ's divine life within us.

The little parable of the wedding garment unfolds a meaning we didn't suspect at first reading. The Mass is the rehearsal and preparation for the Messianic feast. There, every Sunday, the Lord patiently weaves our festive garment. From one week to the next, he purifies us more and more, molding us in his image, increasing the love in us that raises us little by little to his stature, provided, as St. Augustine says, that it is he alone we seek.

5

The Chosen Few

For many are called, but few are chosen.

—Matthew 22:14

Theologians differ on whether many or few will be saved. Some draw more severe conclusions. Others hold a more lenient view.[1] The Church's magisterium hasn't made up its mind, and this is beneficial for us. Believing that the gates of heaven are wide open, we might be tempted to relax our vigilance. The Church's reservation keeps us in both fear and hope, as does Our Lord.

A stranger once asked Jesus the question that haunts us: "Lord, will those who are saved be few?" The Master replied, also addressing the disciples around him: "Strive to enter by the narrow door; for many, I tell you, will seek to enter and will not be able" (Lk 13:23–24). Jesus did not think it necessary to satisfy

1. The subject is treated in all its breadth by Frederick W. Faber (who firmly supports the merciful view) in *The Creator and the Creature*, book three, chapter two (TAN Books, 1988).

his questioner's curiosity. Divine justice and mercy are equally infinite. We cannot penetrate their mystery. One thing is within our grasp: to take the narrow gate that leads to salvation.

For there are many—however few, there will always be too many—who will not pass through it. Let us imitate Jesus, who wants all to be saved. It would be pointless to tell him that he has saved ninety-nine sheep. If he loses one, it's enough to disturb his rest. He won't have peace until he's found the hundredth. Let's not worry about counting the flock; the Good Shepherd knows which one is missing. And it is, perhaps, me. This is the only problem that we must solve.

The Elect Belong to the Earth

Who are the few chosen, the few elect? The Savior's words certainly don't refer to those in heaven whom we now refer to as "the elect." In apostolic literature, as in the vocabulary of the Gospel, the "elect" belong to the earth. Thus St. Peter writes to the elect "of the Dispersion" (1 Pt 1:1), those Jews throughout the empire who embraced the faith of Jesus Christ and form a holy nation, "a chosen race" (1 Pt 2:9). For his part, St. Paul asks in his Epistle to the Romans: "Who shall bring any charge against God's elect?" (Rom 8:33).

These chosen ones, he specifies, are those sanctified by the grace of Jesus Christ. Paul leaves Titus in Crete "to further the faith of God's elect" (Ti 1:1). He urges the Colossians to be kind to one another, as befits "God's chosen ones" (Col 3:12). Captive for the second time, on the eve of undergoing martyrdom in Rome, he writes to Timothy: "I endure everything for the sake of the elect, that they also may obtain the salvation which in Christ Jesus goes with eternal glory" (2 Tm 2:10). As we can see, all these "elect" or "chosen" are still on earth: They are those who have been admitted to the Church.

A reading of the Gospel leads us to the same conclusion. Apart from the saying that concerns us here, Our Lord mentions the "elect" several times. These too are not yet in heaven. They are his present-day disciples. When they are persecuted for righteousness' sake, let them seek refuge in prayer: "And will not God vindicate his elect, who cry to him day and night? Will he delay long over them? I tell you, he will vindicate them speedily" (Lk 18:7–8).

When Jesus announces the calamities of the last times, he assures us that "for the sake of the elect those days will be shortened," that is, for the sake of Christians living at that time (Mt 24:22). So-called messiahs, false prophets, will add to the confusion of this time: They will perform wonders “so as to lead astray, if possible, even the elect” (Mt 24:24). These elect, who are still in danger of going astray, are indeed on earth. Moreover, at the signal of the great trumpet, the Son of Man, coming on the clouds in power and glory, will send the angels to “gather his elect from the four winds” (Mt 24:31).

In short, whenever the New Testament speaks of the “elect,” it never refers to those in heaven. Jesus was thinking of those living in this world—of the children of Israel, most of whom would reject his message—yet among them, some who would follow him to the end of the world. Called to become disciples, they would be more numerous, alas, than those who would actually become disciples. But then, his lesson is absolutely relevant today: “God our Savior . . . desires all men to be saved and to come to the knowledge of the truth” (1 Tm 2:3–4). God wants to save everyone, and he has not chained his grace to the only means of salvation he instituted. Nevertheless, his Church remains the normal way to him. Many are called to join. But how many can call themselves Christians?

Put aside the vast majority of people who have yet to answer Christ’s call. For now, let’s stick to the countries of Christian civilization. Consider the apostates and neo-pagans who have broken with Christianity, the nominal Christians deprived of all sacramental life, and the baptized who so quietly dispense with the Church. Compare this number with the faithful who participate in the life of Jesus Christ and profess to submit their conduct to his commandments. Are they not, compared to all humanity, the few? The mustard seed has grown since the Lord rose from the grave; but it is far from reaching the size of a tree. True Christians, as we have defined them, are only a minority.

Let's start by acknowledging this fact, but without letting it throw us into an inferiority complex. "Fear not, little flock" said Jesus, and indicated the reason for our confidence: "for it is your Father's good pleasure to give you the kingdom" (Lk 12:32). A double feeling of humility and gratitude should come over us at the thought that, without any merit of our own, we possess the privilege of knowing Jesus Christ and of sharing in his life. The few, yes; but *pauci electi,* a small elite. By an entirely gratuitous favor, we are that portion that God has "chosen" for himself. As the Lord declared: "You did not choose me, but I chose you": *Ego elegi vos,* I have made you an elite (Jn 15:16).

He unites us to himself as closely as branches are attached to the vine. "I am the true vine, and my Father is the vinedresser . . . you are the branches" (Jn 15:1–5). As the branches live from the sap of the vine, so we receive life from Jesus Christ. Abiding in him, we bear fruits of holiness. To this first obligation, the Master adds another: "I chose you and appointed you that you should go and bear fruit and that your fruit should abide" (Jn 15:16).

Belonging to the small elite imposes on us first and foremost the duty to take our Christianity seriously. We can do this by deepening our understanding of its doctrine and principles and striving for holiness and justice. Following in the footsteps of Jesus, the small elite must free themselves from the lusts of pride and money, free their bodies and minds from all bondage, and set out on the road of pure, free, and daring love!

We Cannot Isolate Ourselves from the World

The "few chosen" should not, however, isolate themselves from the "many called" or imagine that they are better than others because they have received more. They have no more merit for being children of the kingdom than the rest of humanity has inherent responsibility. In contrasting these two numerically unequal categories, the Savior did not mean to make a simple mathematical statement. Still less would he allow the chosen ones to become proud so that they "despised others" (Lk 18:9). Some who do not know him, if they received the graces we have, would serve him better than we. The saying *many called, few chosen* (see Mt 22:14), must arouse our remorse, because it contains an order of evangelical conquest. We must go out and "make disciples of all nations" (Mt 28:19).

It is not that our own sanctification is unimportant. The salvation of our soul deserves all our efforts. But it's not just one soul—your soul—that God created with such care. It's not just one soul—your soul—for which Jesus Christ shed all his blood. It's millions and millions of souls, as dear to the three divine Persons as yours. The small elite, as Jesus conceives it, is not a selection of privileged people who devote themselves solely to the work of their personal salvation.

It is necessary that a few practice the evangelical counsels in their purest state. They are the contemplative orders. Their function is to purify and sanctify the Church, while their example guides Christian society toward a more perfect realization of the evangelical counsels. But the monastic state, (which is not, moreover, a specific institution of Christianity) lies outside the existence that God wants for most people. Usually, people are called to the duties of family and social life. A small elite, by the very fact of its divine election, has obligations toward the large number of called, but not yet chosen, people. This obligation requires us to maintain close contact with them. The elite are the salt that must preserve and flavor the world. They are the light that must enlighten it. They are the ferment that hides and mixes within the mass to penetrate and lift it up.

As salt is made to add flavor, a lamp to shine, and leaven to ferment, so a Christian is made to "Christianize." Christians—a small elite—must continue the work of Jesus Christ, extending the kingdom of God among their brethren in daily commerce with everyone they meet. This is done no less by individual encounters than by efforts to Christianize the customs, institutions, and laws of civil life. Their job is not so much to talk as to attend to "the work to which I have called them" and exercise their influence as Christians (Acts 13:2). True Christians are called to work with the "many" to propose and bring to fruition initiatives and solutions imbued with the spirit of the Gospel (Lk 13:24). Wherever the Lord has placed them, they have to think and live as Christians, whether individually or as part of a group. By genuinely living as Christians, they witness to Christ by their actions and make his teachings known through example. From here, they will be able to reveal God's name and share their secret with searching minds. This second action is called the apostolate properly, and it normally comes after one's good example.

Are we faithful to our dual mission of holiness and evangelization? We must neither separate ourselves from the world nor borrow anything unholy from it. May the Lord, who prescribes this task for us, help us to fulfill it, so that through us he may increase the number of his chosen on earth!

6

The Little Way of Saint Thérèse

Unless you turn and become like children, you will never enter the kingdom of heaven.

—Matthew 18:3

St. Thérèse of the Child Jesus spent just under a quarter of a century on earth. There were no major events to mark her short life, either before her early entry into Carmel or during her nine years of cloistered life. Yet Thérèse has won the hearts of Catholics all over the world. With unusual haste, she was raised to the altars twenty-six years after her death. For her, the ordinary deadlines were shortened, the canonical process simplified and, in an unprecedented move since canonizations have been governed by law, she was beatified and canonized by the same Pope. How can we explain such eagerness, if not by the importance of that young Carmelite's message? Thérèse conveyed this message to the Christian people in a short piece of writing she wrote two years before her death at the request of her elder sister. It was never intended for publication: *The Story of a Soul.*

The Story of a Soul is a simple narrative. In it, Sr. Thérèse innocently describes the path that led her to God. She wanted to be nothing more than a little child in the hands of the Father, and live with the humility, carefreeness, and trust of a child. While human weakness and frailty sadden most people, her imperfections didn't discourage her. Being too small, in her own opinion, to climb the rugged staircase of perfection, she saw the arms of Jesus as the "elevator" that would lift her to heaven.[1] On her deathbed, she confided to her prioress that her mission was about to begin. She was to teach souls her "little way" of spiritual childhood.

The Way of Childhood

Sr. Thérèse did not invent a new spirituality. The author of the way of childhood is Our Lord in person: "Unless you turn and become like children, you will never enter the kingdom of heaven" (Mt 18:3). It was on the road to Capernaum that the discussion arose among the apostles, who were walking some distance away from Jesus.

1. Thérèse of Lisieux, *The Story of a Soul,* ed. Mother Agnes of Jesus, trans. Michael Day (TAN Books, 2010), p. 117.

Not long before, the Lord had appointed Cephas to be the future head of his Church. They had reason to believe that Jesus would complete the hierarchy of his kingdom by assigning other honorary functions. So, they began to argue about "who was the greatest" (Mk 9:34). But once inside the house, they remained piteously silent when Jesus asked them: "What were you discussing on the way?" (Mk 9:33). There was no hiding anything from the Lord. Not wishing to add to their embarrassment, Jesus did not insist on their answer. Instead, he called to himself a little child, whom he embraced and placed in their midst.

It would be a caricature of the Savior's thinking to imply that infantilism is helpful for the faithful. His revelation is addressed to mature and thoughtful minds. St. Paul warned the faithful of Corinth against the childishness they tolerated in their liturgical assemblies: "Do not be children in your thinking" he wrote to them, "be babes in evil, but in thinking be mature" (1 Cor 14:20). The Christian has adult judgment, but a child's heart.

The way of childhood is a way of living that requires a mature disposition. Little children can't do anything on their own. They expect everything from their father. They know that their father loves them and will give them what they need. They ask him with the certainty of being listened to. Little children don't worry about anything, and they believe what their father tells them. To become like a little child again is to keep this same attitude toward God, and to serve him in a spirit of simplicity and total trust. This simplicity excludes scruples and fear as much as self-interested calculations. Little children let themselves be led, even if sometimes they cry out and struggle because they're suffering. Christians aren't impassive under trial, but instead of complaining about God, they count on God to alleviate their sufferings. Finally, total trust, because it is inspired by love, implies a complete stripping away of our personal preferences with a prompt and joyful abandonment to God's plans. All Christians must enter into a spirit of abandonment, in spite of their passing infidelities.

A Simple but Demanding Path

To hear Thérèse speak of abandonment with such ease, one might be mistaken and conclude that the path of childhood leads to perfection without difficulties. This is not so. It is the simplest and quickest route, but it's not an easy one. Like the royal way of the cross, it demands absolute obedience to all divine demands. We know that the young saint was not spared her trials. The smile under which she hid her sufferings only underlines her heroic endurance. Her illness caused her extreme pain. She froze to death in her cell, coughed up blood, could barely stand, but she refused any relief. Did she at least find compensation in a serene tranquility of soul? On the contrary, she was overwhelmed by inner anguish: aridity and desolation in prayer, temptations against her faith, misunderstandings on the part of some of her sisters. It was in this desert and through these obstacles that she sang of God's love.

The way of childhood does not exempt us from self-denial. Jesus makes this an absolute rule for those who want to follow him. We cannot find God without feeling the hardships of sacrifice. The power of the way of childhood is this: that the rigors of obedience are softened by a stronger sense of God's paternal tenderness. This is what Thérèse highlighted, and this insight—entirely in line with Gospel teaching—changes the game for spiritual struggle and progress. The emphasis is no longer on self-imposed privations, but on the resulting enrichment. Because they know they are loved, children of God aspire to prove their love too. And if they suffer at the renunciations by which they provide these proofs, they derive from them the far greater joy of loving God more.

But at the end of her life, in the throes of the worst pain, she would say quite simply: "I do not repent of having delivered myself up to Love."[2] Our Lord's words reecho: "Unless you turn and become like children . . ." (Mt 18:3). Jesus gives us no choice: It's take it or leave it. If we have recognized the truth of his words, all we have to do is let him shape us in his own image, surrendering ourselves as he did to the Father's will, and devoting ourselves as he did to the service of our brothers and sisters.

Let there be no more talk of our misery! St. Thérèse taught us to accept our own smallness. She showed us how to achieve perfection by fulfilling our daily duties under God's gaze and enduring our daily trials. She assured us that "little souls" must be able to succeed in imitating her. Alas, our poor souls are even smaller than the young saint imagined, judging by the difficulty we have in abandoning ourselves to God. When will we stop commanding and resisting and simply let ourselves be led by the Lord, without worrying about the bumps in the road or the detours along the way? Do we give in to pride or fear? Perhaps both, but we can free ourselves from both by substituting love. But let's at least begin by taking the first steps on the road to childhood, repeating after St. Thérèse—and we can do so in all sincerity: "I want to love you, Lord, like a little child!"

---

2. Thérèse of Lisieux, *The Last Conversations of Saint Thérèse of Lisieux*, ed. Mother Agnes of Jesus (The Neumann Press, 1998), p. 138.

7

The Days Are Evil

> Look carefully then how you walk, not as unwise men but as wise, making the most of the time, because the days are evil.
>
> —Ephesians 5:15–16

There's no excuse for wasting the time God gives us to accomplish our life's work. However, the Apostle offers a special motive to use time well, namely that "the days are evil." Note the Latin text of Paul's epistle: *redimentes tempus.* It's a question of "redeeming the evil of the days," of making better use of them, the worse they are. But what are these "evil days?" There are several plausible meanings, each with its own lesson.

The bad days are usually the ones we live in. People's traditions place the golden age in the distant origins of their civilizations. What moralist of any era has not denounced the mores of his time as if there had never been worse? It's only human nature to dwell on unfortunate things that happen, while we enjoy the relative tranquility of happy days without appreciation.

This commonplace moralizing cannot be attributed to St. Paul when he laments that "the days are evil." The Apostle wrote the letter to the Ephesians during his first captivity in Rome, where, although a prisoner in the Lord's cause, he enjoyed a semi-freedom which he used to preach the Gospel. The days to which he refers are not yet those of the persecution that Nero will soon unleash against Christians, convinced less of their burning Rome, as Tacitus says, than of their "hatred of the human race."[1] But could Paul not discern the early signs of popular hostility against the new religion? At the very least, he suffered at the lamentable spectacle of the pagans of Rome. Given as they were to wine and debauchery, they continually refused the message of Christ. These are sad days he is spending among them, and they foreshadow worse ones to come. It is urgent that Christians of all churches redouble their fervor and intensify their apostolate.

You may feel that our days are also "evil days." If we were to confine ourselves to human calculations, we'd be close to despondency, huddled together awaiting death. St. Paul tells us that such resignation would be sinful. That the present times are evil is even more reason to do

1. Tacitus, *Annals* 15.44, trans. John Jackson (Harvard University Press, 1937).

good. Let us redeem the evil through works of faith and charity. Let us make the most of our time.

The crucial reason to make the most of our time is that our days are numbered. We need to make the most of the time we have left to beg God's mercy and join the righteous who observe his law. We sing the song of the exiled Israelites, weeping along the rivers of Babylon, longing for the day when they will return to their homeland.

All these songs create an atmosphere that gives the Apostle's "evil days" their final, true meaning. These "evil days" are the days of distress that precede the Parousia. They are the days that precede our death: the days of sickness, old age, and infirmity. These days are the harbingers of judgement. Because our time will surprise us "like a thief," we must be ready for departure, so that this unpredictable day will not be a day of misfortune (1 Thes 5:2). The deadline draws nearer as we grow older. Let's take advantage of this time to make up for our past negligence. If our waning strength limits our apostolate, perhaps our experience will make our action more fruitful.

Euphoria of the Spirit

Whatever the application given to the "evil days" of which St. Paul speaks, the means he indicates for correcting their malice do not vary. "And do not get drunk with wine, for that is debauchery; but be filled with the Spirit" (Eph 5:18).

At first glance, Paul's connection is surprising. Is there any relationship, even of contrast, between wine and grace? Don't be fooled into thinking that this was just a joke slipped into the letter, for the same contrast can be seen in the angel's message to Zechariah about the birth and mission of John the Baptist: "He will be great before the Lord," says the heavenly messenger, "he shall drink no wine nor strong drink, and he will be filled with the Holy Spirit" (Lk 1:15). What's more, on Pentecost when the 120 disciples leave the Upper Room, proclaiming the glory of the risen Christ, passers-by are struck with amazement and many, quick to scoff, sneer: "They are filled with new wine" (Acts 2:13). Peter cuts the slander short: "These men are not drunk . . . but this is what was spoken by the prophet Joel: 'And in the last days it shall be, God declares, that I will pour out my Spirit upon all flesh'" (Acts 2:15–17).

These two Scripture passages shed light on St. Paul's recommendation. The action of the Holy Spirit in souls creates a fervor that is comparable to the euphoria of wine. And yet, in evil days, we may be tempted to drink for a stimulant or oblivion. This is a recipe for disaster. The help we need is the Holy Spirit. Let us make God the offering of our times, presenting our work and our rest to him, as well as our joys and our sorrows. In this way, the darkest, hardest, and most monotonous days will become useful, sanctifying, and meritorious days, brightened by the Holy Spirit.

8

Waiting For a Miracle

> Unless you see signs and wonders you will not believe.
>
> —John 4:48

At Capernaum an official's son was ill. When he heard that Jesus had come from Judea to Galilee, he went and begged him to come down and heal his son, for he was at the point of death. Jesus therefore said to him, "Unless you see signs and wonders you will not believe." The official said to him, "Sir, come down before my child dies." Jesus said to him, "Go; your son will live" (Jn 4:46–50).

Only a hasty reading of the fourth chapter of John would give the impression that, after refusing to see the royal official, Our Lord changed his mind and agreed to perform the miracle requested. Jesus begins by rebuking those who need signs and wonders *before* believing in him. The Savior did not correct his earlier condemnation. The official *believed before he saw.* He will be rewarded, firstly by his child's healing, and even more so by the grace to become a disciple of the Lord.

Moreover, the reproach was formulated in the plural. It was aimed at all those present: "*Unless you see signs and wonders.*" In reality, the many miracles performed by Jesus were part of his messianic function. The prophets had foretold him, and these wonders were necessary to win his disciples. Nonetheless, his miracles produced few conversions. Jesus complained about this on several occasions. He reproached the inhabitants of Chorazin and Bethsaida, where the greatest number of his miracles had taken place, for not converting (Mt 11:21); and of the people of Jerusalem, he said: "If I had not done among them the works which no one else did, they would not have sin" (Jn 15:24). St. John notes with sadness: "Though he had done so many signs before them, yet they did not believe in him" (Jn 12:37).

Miracles do not, of themselves, produce faith. Miracles shock onlookers to shake up their routine. If internal prejudices don't stand in the way, miracles strengthen nascent, confused, or wavering faith. It is because Jesus finds faith that he heals so many sick people. His words are well known: "Great is your faith! Be it done for you as you desire." (Mt 15:28). Because of the unbelief in Nazareth, however, Jesus couldn't perform any miracles among them, except a few healings: "He marveled because of their unbelief" (Mk 6:6). Jesus also proclaimed that, one day, an evil and adulterous generation would only be granted the "sign" of the prophet Jonah: the image of his resurrection from the dead (Mt 12:39). After the initial, dazzling proof of his divinity, all that would remain is belief in his word. "Blessed are those who have not seen and yet believe" (Jn 20:29).

Let's come back to our time and to ourselves. One might think that the progress of science would discourage people from looking elsewhere than nature for wonders. But the taste for the marvelous has not been exorcised yet. Especially in times of hardship, apparent prophets abound, and many people listen. Similarly, at the first rumors of apparitions, large numbers of people stir, and they yield only reluctantly to the reservations or prohibitions of ecclesiastical authority.

Spectacles are still seducing people's minds. There are still some who, in the "evil days" we are living through, implore the "sign" from heaven that will expose and destroy the ideologies set up against Christian truth, making them burst forth before everyone's eyes. On a smaller scale, others hope for a miracle to convert an unbelieving relative who rebels against their influence.

No doubt these "faithful" have excellent intentions, but don't they remember Jesus's warning at the end of one of his parables? When the rich man begs Abraham to send Lazarus down to his five brothers to tell them of his suffering, the Patriarch replies: "They have

Moses and the prophets; let them hear them." And the rich man insists: "No, father Abraham; but if some one goes to them from the dead, they will repent." Abraham replies, "If they do not hear Moses and the prophets, neither will they be convinced if some one should rise from the dead" (Lk 16:29–31). Moses and the prophets have made it clear enough to the unfortunate man's brothers. There are consequences for misusing wealth. Without faith in the Word of God, even a miracle as sensational as the dead rising will not persuade them. Their opposition to faith stems not from ignorance but from prejudice or evil dispositions. This sort of obstacle cannot be removed by miracles.

The False Hope of Signs and Wonders

This is all the more reason why we should not place our hope in signs and wonders, or risk our faith by stubbornly insisting on them. One Christian man asked God for a miracle to save a loved one from illness. When the inevitable death came, this man stopped praying and believing. Of course, the Lord doesn't disapprove of the boldest prayers. "All things are possible to him who believes," he declared (Mk 9:23). However, the most admirable faith is that which believes without miracles. This faith repeats the words of our Savior in

Gethsemane: "Father, if thou art willing, remove this cup from me; nevertheless not my will, but thine, be done" (Lk 22:42).

Other Christians feel their faith extinguished because God denies them the miracle of keeping a loved one from a life of sin, or the miracle of preventing a child from contracting a deplorable marriage, or the miracle of averting the ruin of a business. "Yet," they explain, "we had prayed with all our faith. God did not hear us. Is there a God who hears us?"

Is that all your faith is? Rather, beg the Lord to "help my unbelief" (Mk 9:24). For, if you believe that God is your Father, just as he is the Father of those you have prayed for, then you must be certain that his providence guards them. If God must respect their freedom, his grace will still follow them in their errors and misfortunes. He will use their sad experiences or trials to bring them back to himself. This is the true "miracle" reserved for your faith, for all things are possible to him who believes.

Souls of faith don't need signs or wonders to believe in God's presence. They recognize God's action in the most banal incident as well as in the most spectacular miracle. When God modifies the usual play of natural forces, is his action more evident than in the regular course of the universe?

The Christian in the habit of daily adoration easily discovers God's action in the world. What could be more beautiful than to see vegetation spring up again each time spring returns! The Creator is faithful to his children. He doesn't forget them; he will nourish them again this year. This marvel shows us, of course, that God is in our midst. Deceived by empty words, we are always in his arms. The progress of science, to which nature reveals its secrets one by one, makes us increasingly aware of God's perfect, divine works.

Chance Encounters

To the eyes of a believer, divine intervention is clear in any sequence of events. Sometimes, events play out so differently from what was foreseen that people call them "miracles." Let's reserve this term for the great, happy events of history. Still, who among us has not had, at least once in their life, their own "miracle"? You left home at an unusual hour, or you took an unusual route; you made an encounter and said the yes or no that determined a momentous event, to which you owe the happiness of your life. A real miracle, you say? God never ceases to perform similar ones for all his children.

You object that another time some chance encounter or unexpected decision caused you an accident or misfortune. *Was the Father watching over us then?*—Don't doubt it. If you believe before you've seen signs and wonders, you won't rush to regret misfortunes. They may be painful, but they are only one stage in your existence. God knows the twists and turns and the end of the road on which his goodness accompanies you.

There are deep secrets between God and the believer. An inner light affirms God's presence within us, and God's inner presence changes us from day to day. This is the same call we read in the Gospels: "Repent . . . follow me" (Mt 4:17–19). When a sinner converts, or an apostate suddenly returns to the faith, these are the intrusions of a Person who turns our ideas upside down and upsets our desires. These are miracles of a moral nature that are more astonishing and persuasive than any external wonder.

All miracles, apparitions, and spiritual favors pale in comparison with the Incarnation, that unheard-of gift of God "who did not spare his own Son but gave him up for us" (Rom 8:32). We clamor for miracles when we have received infinitely more. We would like God to make events follow the slope of our dreams, and we close our eyes to the supernatural wonders that his power works in us. Let us accept our human condition, with all its obscurities, trials, and sufferings. And still yet another miracle awaits us at the end of these "evil days" as well. We are on our way to eternal life!

9

Witnesses to Jesus Christ

I became your father in Christ Jesus through the gospel. I urge you, then, be imitators of me.

—1 Corinthians 4:15–16

The joy of being a Christian is only truly enjoyed when shared with others. The isolated Christian does not exist. The Christian is a member of Christ, part of his Church, and it is as such that he will stand before God. However, the security of belonging to the Church imposes on us a correlative duty to work for its growth and perfection. By granting us salvation, Jesus Christ obliges us to go beyond concern for our own individual fate and extend the kingdom of God on earth.

We learn this lesson from the first bishop of France, St. Denis. When all the Church is resurrected, "at the voice of the archangel," it is he who will lead the Parisian Church to meet the Lord (1 Thes 4:16). From heaven, our leader is reviewing his troops, inspecting the new recruits he wants to lead to victory, and seeing what his Church has become. He presents to our eyes the martyrdom he endured for Jesus Christ, so that "imitating his faith" we add our testimony to his.

One day, in France, this man proclaimed for the first time the Gospel of Jesus Christ, Son of God. This fact has left its mark on history. After all, Christianity, born in Palestine, could just as easily have spread first to the countries of the East, in which case the people lost at the very tip of Europe would have remained ignorant of the true God for centuries. But because Rome was the metropolis of the civilized world, the missionaries of the Gospel went west.

By the middle of the third century, Gaul's religious foundations rested on two layers of differing depth. The deeper layer was naturalistic polytheism. The piety of the Gaulish people divinized the forces of nature. In their defense, they did not represent their gods with human features, but only symbolic pictures. They particularly venerated the mysterious powers that constantly fed their springs and rivers, as well as woodland divinities. The cult of trees led to the famous gathering of mistletoe. Not being the normal fruit of the oak, mistletoe seemed to have a marvelous origin, while its perpetual greenness symbolized immortality. Mistletoe could only be cut on the first day of the lunar month by the golden sickle of the white-robed druids.

These druids were a perfectly organized clergy, with their own hierarchy, novitiate, and regular assemblies. They professed a very firm doctrine on the future life, taught morality, and oversaw its observance, for they themselves exercised justice. I mention these details only to explain why St. Thomas Aquinas pointed to Gallic Druidism as the providential preparation for a land where "Christian priesthood should especially thrive."[1] The Roman conquest dealt a mortal blow to the ancient religion of the Gauls. Tiberius could not be blamed for forbidding human sacrifice, but the shrewd politician, who saw in the druids an authority rivaling his own, ordered its dissolution. With the druids gone, the Roman deities superimposed, and then replaced, the Celtic gods. This second, inferior, layer of paganism led to religious regression. Especially in urban areas, the people, without yet shedding their barbarism, assimilated Roman civilization with all its decadent vices.

It was this two-fold paganism that Denis had to face when he pitched his tent on the outskirts of the charming little town of Lutetia, modern day Paris. The natives first observed that this stranger was neither official nor merchant. He lived modestly and made himself loved.

---

1. Thomas Aquinas, *On Kingship to the King of Cyprus*, trans. and ed. Ignatius Eschmann (Pontifical Institute of Mediaeval Studies, 1949), book 2, chap. 3.

To some, he confided that he was the messenger of Jesus Christ: "A new God? No, the one, true God who became man to make us sons of God." Who wouldn't raise an eyebrow at such assertions? Many, however, were persuaded, for the holiness of this Dionysius seemed to betoken his sincerity.

Denis's speeches, however, aroused the suspicions of the majority. To those who believed what their ancestors believed, Denis declared that they were in error and that Christ must replace their false gods. What's more, he refrained from burning incense before the emperor's image, and he preached a lifestyle that upset their habits. His Christ condemned polygamy, lying, avarice. . . .

Aurelian's edict outlawing Christian worship put a timely end to the activities of this gentle stranger and his severe doctrine. Denis was denounced along with two other Christians. The number of baptized the bishop had gathered to celebrate the mysteries was small. How many followers had he made? Evidently enough to bear witness and establish Christianity definitively among Parisians. The three accused refused to sacrifice in the temple of Mercury, and they were arrested on the spot. Under the axe that cut off his head, Bishop Denis gave a final proof of his faith. Rather than deny his creed, he preferred to die.

Let us carefully weigh the value of this testimony. The death of martyrs does not establish the truth of a doctrine, since men can sacrifice their lives for erroneous convictions. Martyrdom does, however, prove the truth of a historical fact. Martyrs are "witnesses," and one can only bear witness to a fact. Pascal wrote: "I believe only the histories (not ideas) whose witnesses (not supporters) got themselves killed."[2]

Our Christian faith is based on a historical fact, the fact of Jesus's resurrection, supreme proof of his divinity. The apostles were eyewitnesses to this fact, and they were willing to die to attest to their certainty. The apostles' disciples in turn testified to this certainty. From one generation to the next, our martyrs offer themselves up to death, not only because they are convinced of the truth of Christian doctrine, but to guarantee the facts of the divinity of Jesus Christ on which our faith rests.

It's worth noting that Christianity was never introduced into a pagan land without missionaries bearing witness through blood. The workers of the Redemption follow in the Savior's footsteps, mingling their sacrifice with his. The grain of wheat must fall into the earth and die there in order to bear fruit. A few years before

---

2. Blaise Pascal, *Pensées*, trans. W. F. Trotter (Dover Publications, 2018), section 9.592, p. 163.

the martyrdom of St. Denis, Tertullian, in Africa, braved the persecuting magistrates with his customary ardor: "Do your worst, and rack your inventions for tortures for Christians—it is all to no purpose . . . the more you mow us down, the thicker we rise; the Christian blood you spill is like the seed you sow."[3] The blood of the first three Parisian martyrs bore fruit. Today, the basilica, from which uninterrupted adoration rises to God, stands on the summit of the "martyrs' mountain" (Montmartre), overlooking the domes and bell towers of the city.

The small Christian community of the ninth century became one of the most famous churches in Christendom, the Church of St. Genevieve and St. Louis. In the Middle Ages, while war and battle raged in Rome, the University of Paris was commonly referred to as "the permanent council of the Gauls." When schism tore Christendom apart, it was from Paris that Jean Gerson led the fight for the unity of the Church. Alas, this providential warning was not heeded, and the religious reform called for by the saints was always postponed. God then allowed the painful secession of Protestantism, which tore away half of Europe from the Holy See. But one night in August 1534, on the eve of the

3. Tertullian, *Apology for Christians*, trans. W. M. Reeve (London: Griffith Farran, n.d.), chap. 50, p. 143.

Assumption, in Sacré-Coeur Basilica, in the chapel erected on the spot where Denis was beheaded, Ignatius of Loyola, Francis Xavier, and five other students from the University of Paris dedicated their lives to the defense of Catholic dogma. The Church of St. Denis, once exemplified by St. Vincent de Paul, experienced sad days during the revolutionary era. Two of its archbishops fell victim to riots, yet it has lost none of its vitality. Now it's up to us to write our own page in this history, if we heed the call of St. Denis: "I urge you, then, be imitators of me" (1 Cor 4:15–16).

We owe much to the prayer, holiness, and sacrifices of previous generations. Let us never be proud of our virtue, as if we had acquired it by our own efforts alone. In addition to the principal part played by grace, it is owed to the merits of others at least as much as our own. We cannot save ourselves in isolation. We are always helped by the prayers of the whole Church and the merits of the saints. We too must strive to help our fellow Christians gain salvation. And how could the problem of evangelizing not arise in our minds? There are many more pagans today than in the time of St. Denis, and pagans who are more recalcitrant to grace, because they are more often apostates. The example of St. Denis teaches us that the witness of our word and life must be built on a life of prayer.

The primary task of Christians is the evangelization of the world. What makes the evangelist's work fruitful is the sacrifice he makes of his life to Jesus Christ. To voluntarily and generously unite to Christ's sacrifice a life of sickness or hardship has immense apostolic value. But all of us can offer a mortified life. This is the total self-gift by which Christians affirm their faith in the death and resurrection of the Savior. We give everything to the One who is everything to us. In so doing, we make the Church holier and more ready to conquer!

10

Spiritual Warfare

> Therefore take the whole armor of God, that you may be able to withstand in the evil day.
>
> —Ephesians 6:13

Reading Paul's Epistle to the Ephesians, we can almost see the astonishment in the eyes of its first listeners. They are slightly unsettled by the symbolism St. Paul draws from the equipment of the Roman legionaries: "Therefore take the whole armor of God" (Eph 6:13). Don't let the imagery distract from the sequence of ideas that the Apostle proposes for our reflection. Let's try to get to the heart of it.

Paul's advice is intended to bolster our courage in the "evil days." The backdrop is always the Parousia, the day when we will leave the land of bondage. The epistle speaks of spiritual warfare. The warning is necessary. We would expose ourselves to bitter disappointment if our confidence in God's mercy became a pretext for slackening our efforts. Perfection cannot be acquired cheaply. The only way to follow Jesus is to renounce mediocrity. Let us not deceive ourselves: Love proves itself only by constant service, self-forgetfulness, and sacrifice.

St. Paul insists on the fierceness of the battle we fight. To heal our sinful nature, we can't merely *defend* ourselves against the seductions of sin. In that case, we would be fighting on equal terms. Our enemies are not of flesh and blood. Every baptized person is the object of the devil's attacks. It is true that the grace of baptism is a grace of martyrdom, and it obliges Christians to "live no longer for themselves but for him who for their sake died and was raised" (2 Cor 5:15). Nevertheless, Christians follow God's will only at the price of continual sacrifice. Satan would easily overcome man's strength unaided, but he cannot stop the Christian who has put his strength in the Lord. This is the second teaching of the epistle: "Finally, be strong in the Lord and in the strength of his might" (Eph 6:10).

Divine help comes from within us. We are united to the Lord's omnipotence in a very real way. However, God wants us to struggle ourselves. He will lead us into battle, but we must benefit from his power by using the divine weapons he gives us.

The Armor of God

Our natural virtues are far from useless, and we need to make the most of them. In the fight against sin, we need to be vigilant and prudent, tenacious and bold. This is why St. Paul, fighting alongside us in the fray, cries out to us: "Take the whole armor of God" (Eph 6:13).

The Apostle often uses images to engrave his thoughts in the memory of his disciples. Above all, he takes his metaphors from the games of the stadium and the profession of arms. Isn't the Christian life a battle? In spiritual warfare, of course, the Christian's weapons "are not worldly" (2 Cor 10:4), but military terms still provide St. Paul with wonderful analogies. He had already advised the Thessalonians to "put on the breastplate of faith and love, and for a helmet the hope of salvation" (1 Thes 5:8). The Epistle to the Ephesians only contains a fuller description of the infantryman's armor:

> Therefore take the whole armor of God, that you may be able to withstand in the evil day, and having done all, to stand. Stand therefore, having girded your loins with truth, and having put on the breastplate of righteousness, and having shod your feet with the equipment of the gospel of peace; above all taking the shield of faith, with which you can quench all the

> flaming darts of the evil one. And take the helmet of salvation, and the sword of the Spirit, which is the word of God. (Eph 6:13–18)

In his prison in Rome, Paul had plenty of time to notice the attire of those guarding him. From the soldiers' shoes tied to his calves, to the helmet which hid his face, and his belt that wrapped around the waist. There was the breastplate on the soldier's chest, and on his left arm there was a bronze shield, trimmed with fresh leather. In his right hand, the legionnaire held a double-edged sword. These became so many images to describe the Christian's spiritual defenses.

Just as the legionnaire, putting on his equipment, began by tightening the folds of his tunic in his belt, so Paul tells the Christian to first "stand . . . having girded your loins with truth" (Eph 6:14). The "Father of Lies" first tries to make us sin by concealing the seriousness of the evil we do, or by persuading us that we have the right to act as we please. If we are determined to obey God nevertheless, he tries to make us doubt our own strength, or inspire us to an excessive esteem for it. This way he can lead us into discouragement or presumption. To this end, he hides our qualities and defects from us, or he exaggerates them. Deceived by these illusions, we commit the negligence or imprudence that is our usual route to sin.

To avoid these traps, St. Paul tells us, Christians must *live in the truth.* Let us seek our rule of conduct in the truth of the Gospel. Every rule is a hindrance. So too is a belt, yet it supports the traveler who must complete a long journey. The law of the Gospel, while restraining us from sin, keeps us moving at a good pace along the true road to goodness. What's more, the truth of the Gospel lets us see ourselves clearly. We consider both our weaknesses and our strengths, and we are able to keep Jesus's word and put it into practice.

Satan then seeks to strike at our hearts, encouraging the selfishness that grips every fiber of our being and is the source of all sin. To quell this false love of ourselves, Jesus commands us to "hunger and thirst for righteousness" (Mt 5:6). The word "justice" here means all the virtues, which are all summed up in love. This is the breastplate that St. Paul invites us to wear, to protect our hearts. Let's wrap ourselves in Christ's love. Christ's charity will justify us in God's eyes and urge us to serve others.

In fact, it is concern for others that the Apostle points to as the third means of bringing our struggle to a successful conclusion. The apostolate helps us remain faithful to Jesus Christ. How can we proclaim the Gospel unless we strive to submit our whole lives to it? Zeal has God as its object. God's love is a jealous love, which does not let us rest until we have made the Lord we love known all around us. Paul's eagerness to proclaim "the gospel of peace" is symbolized by the infantryman's shoes, which are both strength and light (Eph 6:15).

But the "flaming darts of the evil one" are not merciful (Eph 6:16). They must be extinguished immediately. The Romans had fought against enemies who would unexpectedly hurl javelins coated with pitch and resin. These javelins set their targets on fire if not stopped. To protect themselves, the soldiers had a large rectangular shield. The devil's tactics are similar.

Unexpected Tactics of the Enemy

The devil reserves unexpected attacks for the disciples of Christ, and sows panic when least expected. Without any warning, he will unleash the worst temptation of all, that of doubt: *Are you sure that a God is thinking of you? Aren't you giving up the prey for the shadow? If there's nothing after this life, you'll have deprived yourself in vain. The others you'd like to attract to the Gospel, see how they do without. They take life calmly as it comes, while worry gnaws at you. . . .*

Then the disciple stops mid-stride. Will we continue our costly efforts to achieve an illusory or useless perfection? Why not taste the joys that are forbidden to us instead? That's why St. Paul warmly urges us: "above all taking the shield of faith" (Eph 6:16). He says: "above all," because the danger that threatens us then is the most serious. The faith Paul speaks of here is not so much adherence to religious truth, mentioned at the start of the battle, as unreserved attachment to Jesus Christ. For nothing, he writes elsewhere, "in all creation, will be able to separate us from the love of God in Christ Jesus Our Lord" (Rom 8:39). Let us not, in the heat of battle, doubt our Leader and hesitate to follow him. In the droughts or in the dark night, in the hours of weariness or disgust, let us cling to him in spite of everything—in spite of ourselves. He loved us, he gave himself up for us, let us never doubt his love. "For whatever is born of God overcomes the world; and this is the victory that overcomes the world, our faith" (1 Jn 5:4).

Having failed to corrupt the Christian's heart, Satan whispers into his mind. Like a helmet for a legionnaire, the "helmet of salvation" will protect the Christian against the tempter's final blows (Eph 6:17). Jesus has saved us, and our victory is assured provided we don't give up. Let's not fall into defeatism because the war is dragging on. We are sure of victory. The battle is going on just as our Leader planned: contradictions, scorn, tribulations, and persecutions. All this was on the agenda when we enlisted. Victory, too, was promised to us, and it will come as the rest does. Let's hold our heads high and keep the composure we need to make the right decision.

For we are now prepared for the enemy's attacks; the moment has come to go on the offensive. We now enter the hour of hand-to-hand combat, when we will put our adversary out of action. We need only one sword to bring him down, a sword that nothing can break, an enchanted sword that *the Holy Spirit* himself has forged and tempered: "the word of God" (Eph 6:17). Not only the Gospel, the sword is "every word that proceeds from the mouth of God" (Mt 4:4). Our Lord has shown us by his example that the adversary cannot resist this sword. When Satan attacked him three times in the desert, he countered each time with these simple words: "It is written." And the enemy retreated. His tactic—he showed it in the Garden of Eden—is always to make us question God's commands. Any command discussed will soon be transgressed. We don't discuss, we carry out the Lord's commands. God's word compels the armies of error and sin to retreat. "It is written" is the secret of victory.

11

The Measure of Forgiveness

> Then his lord summoned him and said to him, "You wicked servant! I forgave you all that debt because you besought me; and should not you have had mercy on your fellow servant, as I had mercy on you?" And in anger his lord delivered him to the jailers, till he should pay all his debt. So also my heavenly Father will do to every one of you, if you do not forgive your brother from your heart.
>
> –Matthew 18:32–35

The parable of the unforgiving servant brings us before the tribunal where we will meet the Lord. The reckoning has begun. One by one, we pass before our King. Trembling with fear, we fall at his feet, for we cannot repay our debt, and our debt is immense, and the King's sentence will be final.

What will that sentence be? Our Savior has not taken us by surprise. He has warned us in the most explicit terms: We ourselves decide our eternal fate. He will use *the same measure* to judge us as we use to judge others. If we forgive, we shall obtain mercy. If we do not forgive, God will treat us with the utmost rigor.

Let's move on to the lesson of the parable: "He could not pay" (Mt 18:25). Before God, we are all penniless debtors. In the story he told, Jesus intentionally blurred the lines. Kings normally don't lend money to their subjects. Usually, it is the other way around. Moreover, the minister owes the sovereign a truly exorbitant sum: *ten thousand talents*. These incredible details, however, depict our real situation before God. Do we dare compare the service we render God with the immense gifts he gives us? What could we add after saying that he gave us *his Son*? What have we done with so much wealth at our disposal? We have squandered and misused much of it. Our balance sheet is an enormous liability of good wishes unfulfilled, promises forgotten, faults half-considered, and sins consented to. For all this, we deserve to be sentenced "till [we] should pay all [our] debt," and since we never will, we should be condemned to endless punishment.

When God looks at our liabilities, he also sees the other side of the balance sheet and there finds a small residue of charity. Yes, the God we have offended loves us all the same. The pain we feel at our own poor conduct, just as much as, if not more than, the fear of punishment, throws us at his feet: "Lord, have patience with me, and I will pay you everything" (Mt 18:26). And the

King, who knows our weakness and the clay from which we are made, is seized with pity. Because he is just, he judges us with mercy and cancels his claim.

Repentance Before Forgiveness

No doubt God waits for us to repent before forgiving us. All we need do is ask. On his part, he asks only to forgive us. He gives and he forgives, because he is God. But love calls for reciprocity. God only tosses aside our sins if we prove that, despite our disobedience, we wholeheartedly love him. Not just with our lips, but with our hearts. And the way to love God whom we have never seen, writes St. John, is to love our brother whom we do see (1 Jn 4:20). By consenting to make justice yield to mercy, the Lord opens the regions of grace to us. We will only enter them on condition that we imitate him and show mercy.

Thus the judgment that will determine our eternity depends strictly on us. God will measure his forgiveness by our forgiveness toward our brothers and sisters. Isn't this promise a source of deep and wonderful joy? All we have to do is empty our hearts of resentment toward others, and our Father will embrace us in his arms.

It is important to point out that Our Lord is only speaking on the individual level. Jesus is not condemning the legal prosecution that society has a duty to bring against criminals. Our Lord does not take the right of the sword away from legitimate authorities, whose purpose is to guarantee the common good. Failure to repress injustice would be the worst injustice of all. The wrong we suffer may entail necessary consequences for its perpetrator, which we are rarely free to prevent. Depending on whether it's a question of safeguarding justice or peace, we will be authorized to defend our rights or invited to renounce them. Jesus forbids only one thing, but he forbids it absolutely. He forbids it because it violates justice: revenge. Against the always immoderate desire for retaliation, he wants us to forget insults and forgive offenses.

So it's only in the innermost depths of our conscience that the Lord's precept affects us, but in this realm he commands us without limitation. To rule out any excuse whereby we might shelter our grudges, the Savior orders us to compare our brothers' debts to us with our own debts to God. The merciless servant in the parable, just released from a huge debt, seizes one of his fellow servants by the throat and has him thrown into prison because he cannot pay back a trifling sum. A trifle compared to the ten thousand talents the king had forgiven. And the Lord speaks on within us: *What are your brother's shortcomings toward you compared to just one of your sins? Do you refuse to forgive because your honor is at stake? My Father is greater than you, and he forgives.*

I lowered myself to the point of dying on a cross so that you might forgive.

The parable of the unforgiving servant illustrates the Savior's teaching: "If your brother sins, rebuke him, and if he repents, forgive him; and if he sins against you seven times in the day, and turns to you seven times, and says, 'I repent,' you must forgive him" (Lk 17:3–4). Jesus often returns to this obligation: "If your brother sins against you, go and tell him his fault, between you and him alone. If he listens to you, you have gained your brother" (Mt 18:15). Since you're the offended party, you've got the better part. The other is ashamed of their evil deed or harsh word, afraid to appear before you again, and slowly sinking into their wickedness. Go and find them.

Simon Peter, troubled by such a new teaching, wondered if he had understood his Master's meaning: "Lord, how often shall my brother sin against me, and I forgive him? As many as seven times?" And the Savior, with a smile that we can only guess at, extends the hyperbole even further: "I do not say to you seven times, but seventy times seven" (Mt 18:21). By pushing back the limit still further, Jesus does not intend to encourage the guilty party. He considers the case where we have been offended, and radically removes any limit beyond which we might regain the right to hate or to give in to the instinct of revenge.

Forgiveness and Repentance

A Christian must forgive a guilty man who repents. But what if the offender refuses to acknowledge or repair his wrongs? What if he rejects the reconciliation we propose, and, far from repenting, he perseveres in his malignity, continuing to accuse us falsely, tarnish our reputation, and seek to harm us? Is the Lord's precept still binding on us? The sinner must confess his guilt and foster deep sorrow at having transgressed the divine law. Moreover, he is bound to make reparation for his fault, and when it is irreparable, to compensate for it by extra penance. Finally, he must loyally promise not to offend God again. If any of these conditions is lacking, God does not forgive. Logically, aren't we entitled to refuse forgiveness to anyone who doesn't regret the harm or pain he has caused us?

In Christian logic, we must imitate God. But what does God do? He doesn't overwhelm the sinner who persists in his rebellion. He gives us time to mend our ways. God hates evil, but not the wicked. The Christian's behavior can only be helped by divine action. Even though the offender has refused the hand we offer, we stay ready for reconciliation. While condemning evil ways—condemning evil—we leave it to God to judge the wicked, and we forbid ourselves to hate them. The Christian's victory lies in hoping that sinners will repent, and in praying to God that they will be converted from their sins. Our business is not to prolong a grievance or eternalize a dispute, and to that end we try to forget the insult and smother the grudge.

Jesus makes it clear that a transformation must take place within us, whatever the attitude of the guilty party. Forgiveness is not a gesture of indifference. Forgiveness is a sacrifice by which we disarm ourselves so that we can no longer take revenge. And because this sacrifice is costly to our nature, God receives it as atonement for our personal sins and makes it a means of sanctification for us.

Let no one talk to you about forgetting the sin and forgiving the wrongdoers. It's beyond your powers. The one who can make us capable of rising to heroism in forgiveness is the Crucified One on Calvary, who did not want to die before he prayed to the Father to forgive his executioners. Listen to him say again, and try to say again with him: "Father, forgive them . . ." (Lk 23:34).

12

The Salvation of the World

The harvest is plentiful, but the laborers are few.

—Matthew 9:37

Our Lord spoke these words during a journey through the towns and villages of Galilee. The crowds unanimously acclaimed his healings, but they were not prepared to receive his message. They had been abandoned too long by the spiritual leaders of Israel. They seemed to him like a flock of sheep lying on the ground, exhausted after a long travel through arid terrains, with no shepherds to lead them to pasture.

Jesus's heart was stirred with pity. How could he teach them, these victims of religious ignorance? Faced with this challenge, he did not conclude that evil was too great to overcome, and therefore that nothing could be done. Rather, it was time to go to work. These souls were wasting away because they didn't know the truth. Perhaps they could no longer even recognize their spiritual poverty. But if enlightened, they would clamor to enter the kingdom of God. Jesus sees saints in the lost, amorphous crowds.

Look at the present state of the world. The vast majority lives in ignorance. Even Christianity is divided, with disagreement on essential doctrine. Because it has been torn apart, this Christianity has lost control of the mind, and must now relentlessly disengage itself from a materialistic civilization that claims to scientifically justify its atheism. This is the universe we have been given to Christianize. It's a superhuman task, and one that's sure to discourage us. Let us look at it with the eyes of the Savior. For him, these immense zones of paganism are the future lands of his kingdom. The harvest is plentiful. The scale and difficulty of our task only serve to underline its urgency.

All people have the right to know the Good News of salvation. Before he ascends to the Father, Jesus instructs his disciples: "Go into all the world and preach the gospel to the whole creation" (Mk 16:15). He outlines their program of evangelization: they will be his witnesses first in Jerusalem and then in "all Judea and Samaria and to the end of the earth" (Acts 1:8). When the holy city is destroyed and its inhabitants exiled, "the times of the Gentiles" will begin (Lk 21:24). The Lord delays his return, explains St. Peter, "that all should reach repentance" (2 Pt 3:9).

So we have here a formal command from the Lord. After this command, no Christian can accuse missionaries of disturbing nonbelievers who honor the divinity in their own ways. It is not only for pity that missionaries bring the Gospel. Above all, they are fulfilling an act of obedience. Missionaries don't trouble human consciences, they enlighten them. Preachers of the Gospel take great care not to offend the traditions and lifestyles of their neophytes, insofar as they are reconcilable with Christian truth. Missionaries desire only to preach the message of Jesus Christ in its full purity and absolute universality.

Our Lord's imperative mandate dismisses a second objection against missionary action as well: *Don't we have enough work to do here? Let's start by converting the pagans in our own countries, and then we'll deal with the others.*

To heed this suggestion would be to restrict the Church's field of action and, what would be no less serious, drain its conquering power from the present moment in history. The harvest is abundant: It is the size of the earth! We must conquer the whole universe for Jesus Christ. If we lose sight of the totality of the work to be accomplished, our will to evangelize will slow down, even with regard to our own local pagans. Missionary vocations, far from hindering the apostolate in our own countries, stimulate those at home. In the sixteenth century, when the Catholic Church had to heal the wounds inflicted by Protestant defections, it did not hesitate to deprive itself of one of its best workers, St. Francis Xavier, in order to send him to preach the Gospel in India.

Missionary work is less about multiplying individual conversions than planting Christianity in every country. In this way, we create small communities of Christians everywhere, who gradually influence the ideas and customs of their friends. Missionary work aims to teach all nations, Christianize all civilizations. What a delusion it would be to wait until Europe fully returns to Christ before making him known on other continents—when there are souls waiting for him everywhere! Many souls still await the missionaries who will first speak to them of Jesus Christ. Proof of this statement lies in the incredible fervor of young Christians in central Africa. One even wonders whether it's not in recently pagan lands that the Gospel is currently showing its most exuberant vitality. The Lord has not retracted his promise: The harvest will be plentiful, but today, as in his day, the laborers are few and far between.

The world which the Savior assigned to the spiritual conquest of his disciples only yesterday impressed us by its vastness. Today, it amazes us by its smallness. Advances in modern technology have greatly shortened distances on our planet. When Our Lord pointed out the disproportion between the abundant harvest and the small number of laborers, he didn't immediately send them to the rescue of the "lost sheep of the house of Israel" (Mt 10:6). There are more pressing matters than going into the field: "He said to them, 'The harvest is plentiful, but the laborers are few; pray therefore the Lord of the harvest to send out laborers into his harvest'" (Lk 10:2). Faced with an undertaking that is beyond human strength, the Master wants us to begin by measuring our own weakness, to acquire the conviction that God alone ensures the effectiveness of our efforts.

Mission and Unity

In our own day, it is clear that the salvation of the world is linked to the Christian unity so sadly damaged. There is some excuse for those who reject Christianity as the only true religion. It is proclaimed to them by preachers divided even among themselves. Before consummating his sacrifice, the Lord begged his Father to maintain the closest unity within the Church. "That they may all be one," he asked, "so that the world may believe that thou hast sent me" (Jn 17:21). The Lord knows that his Church must remain one for the world to believe in him. The condition is absolute. This division throws us into the most dreadful humiliation. The two causes of the missionary apostolate and the Church's return to unity are one and the same. But by what miracle will God reunite his dismembered Church into a single body, and how can we obtain this miracle other than by frantic, unceasing prayer?

The first preachers of the Gospel among unbelievers necessarily come from Christian countries. This stage may be quite long, but it is only temporary, since the pastors of Christian communities cannot be foreigners indefinitely. The peoples of the East rightly value their civilization. They have an intellectual elite with its own demands and legitimate dignity. Christianity will only have credibility among cultivated minds if it is taught to them by men of their own language, education, and rank. For this reason, the Sovereign Pontiffs wish missionaries to prepare native clergy who will, sooner or later, replace them altogether.

The formation of native priests certainly requires the presence and selflessness of missionaries, but it also presupposes, within the first generations of converts, a work of deepening and rejuvenation that is the fruit of prayer. This is so true that, alongside apostolic workers, our contemplative orders in the West proceed in pagan lands with foundations devoted exclusively to prayer. Our Lord asks all the children of his Church to pray, as this prayer is necessary for the growth of new Christian communities. It is the primary contribution of all Christians to the salvation of the world.

In this respect, we can find no more persuasive example than St. Thérèse of Lisieux, the young, cloistered nun who became the "patroness of the missions," a title that would be paradoxical if prayer were not indeed the most powerful weapon for hastening the conversion of pagans. In the last months of her illness, her doctor ordered a daily fifteen-minute walk in the convent garden. One afternoon, as Thérèse was finding it harder than usual to walk, the nun accompanying her advised sitting down. Thérèse declined the invitation: "I offer every step for some missionary who, far away, is exhausted by his work for souls; I offer my exhaustion to relieve his."[1]

May the salvation of the world and the unity of the universal Church be among our habitual prayer intentions. Jesus pointed them out to us in the text he taught us: "Thy kingdom come" (Mt 6:10). Knowing the price our Savior attaches to the salvation of a soul, won't our hearts beat in unison with his at the sight of the pagan multitudes who don't know him?

---

1. Thérèse of Lisieux, *The Story of a Soul*, p. 170.

13

God and Caesar

> Render therefore to Caesar the things that are Caesar's, and to God the things that are God's.
>
> —Matthew 22:21

The denarius incident recounted in the Gospel took place a few days before Jesus's arrest. His enemies, having sworn themselves to his downfall, wanted to break the popular movement that rose in his favor when he entered the city. So they publicly harassed him with questions, hoping to compromise him in the eyes of both the people and the Roman authorities (Lk 20:20).

After several unsuccessful attempts, they set a new trap: "Is it lawful to pay taxes to Caesar, or not?" (Mk 12:14). In fact, Jesus's contemporaries did pay this tribute, but the question of principle remained open and was discussed in the rabbinical schools. The question, though impolite, was perfidiously clever. If Jesus refused the taxes, he would be denounced to the governor. If not, he would accept Israel's servitude and deny God's sovereignty over his people. He would be discredited in the eyes of the crowd, who would no longer see him as their Messiah.

But the Savior had no difficulty in detecting the ruse. The tribute was to be paid, not with the bronze coins that circulated in Palestine for everyday use, but in good silver denarii minted in the image of Tiberius. "Bring me a coin, and let me look at it," he tells the questioners. They are caught in their own trap, for they immediately draw the denarius in question from their belts, proving that they had gone to the moneychanger to pay the tax. Jesus doesn't take the coin, but he is amused by their debacle: "Whose likeness and inscription is this?" They reply: "Caesar's" (Mk 12:13–17).

The Savior does not hold their answer against them. We can be faithful to God while still submitting to earthly powers in matters of earthly jurisdiction. "Render to Caesar the things that are Caesar's, and to God the things that are God's" (Mk 12:17). His opponents remain silent. This answer, which "amazed" those who witnessed the scene, abolished a thousand-year-old confusion between politics and religion (Mk 12:17). However, the last words are often overlooked: "Render to . . . God the things that are God's" (Mk 12:17).

The Denarius and Our Merits

The merits we acquire on earth are the denarius we will render to God on the day of judgement. Sinners who have the misfortune to die in a state of open and voluntary rebellion against God cannot claim an asset of previous good works: Their rebellion has annulled them. When God forgives repentant sinners, however, he returns to them, with his friendship, the merits they had acquired while living in a state of grace. It follows from this that, while avoiding fully-consented sin, we should try to multiply our virtuous actions in the state of grace. God is willing to consider these as "merits," and they will earn us a greater share in his glory.

"Render to . . . God the things that are God's" (Mk 12:17). What will we give him back when we appear before him? Obviously, what belongs to him and what he lent us. In common parlance, "we will return our soul to God." Our soul is created in his image, and baptism has highlighted the inscription of his Son: "Whose likeness and inscription is this?" (Mk 12:13–17). Will the image of Christ be clear? Or will the inscription be erased? Is a counterfeit coin that even Caesar wouldn't want all we have to give God?

Will I have taken care to lead this life that God has given me as uprightly, as benevolently, as he wanted? Five talents, or two, or just one, it doesn't matter how many he has given me, but what I have done with them. Will this diary of my life, despite its inevitable flaws, be a faithful version of the Gospel, or will I hear the judge's appraisal: "Why do you call me 'Lord, Lord,' and not do what I tell you?" (Lk 6:46).

"Render to . . . God the things that are God's" (Mk 12:17). He is Love and he loves us with an eternal love. He loved our poor world so much that he gave it his only Son. Jesus, charity incarnate, loved us to the point of excess, to the point of transforming us into himself in the Eucharist. He did this so that we may know how to love the Father by loving our brothers and sisters as he loved us. And when others see our good deeds, they will glorify the Father in heaven.

The holiness that God's justice requires of us at the end of our earthly life is first and foremost the work of his mercy. "I am sure," St. Paul writes, "that he who began a good work in you will bring it to completion at the day of Jesus Christ" (Phil 1:6). Our part in our own sanctification is very small, but it is indispensable. We must acquiesce to God's love for us.

Close Union with Jesus

"Do you love me?" This question Jesus asks Peter three times after he faltered in his trial. It is also addressed to each and every one of us. The Savior asks us nothing more: "Do you love me?" (Jn 21:15). And our share in our sanctification is contained in our response: *Lord, you who know everything, you know that I love you.* This danger, which does not escape St. Paul's clear-sightedness, prompts him to pray to God on behalf of his beloved Philippians, "that your love may abound more and more" (Phil 1:9).

Charity is close union with Jesus and, through him, with the Holy Trinity. Supernatural life never ceases to grow, as long as the Christian does not fall into mortal sin. Its growth is unlimited: We can always love God more, and unite ourselves with him more closely. This growth, encouraged by the sacraments, is also encouraged by the acts of love performed by the Christian in a state of grace. "Do you love me?" We will prove it to him by refusing him nothing that our reason, enlightened by faith, suggests to us as God's present will.

Progress in charity is possible for everyone. Sanctity is not attached to extraordinary deeds. The humble actions of our days sanctify us as soon as they are offered to God as a tribute of our love, whereas ostentatious almsgiving and fasting lose all merit when they are not offered to the Father in secret. In the same way, we don't overcome our selfishness by seeking to do what we don't like (let's fear the revenge of self-love), but by loving what we must do and what God asks of us. The meritorious value of an act is not necessarily linked to the magnitude of its difficulty. Merit lies first and foremost in the love of the person who acts, whatever he or she does. The Blessed Virgin did not commit the slightest sin. Would we dare suppose that obedience cost her anything? The incomparable quality of her merits lies in that of her love.

The light of the Gospel and the wisdom of the Church will help Christians to accurately perceive the inner counsel of the Holy Spirit. If a false prudence tries to deceive us, we have an infallible clue: Anything is suspect that tends to turn us in on ourselves and avoid costly effort.

Striving to discern the "best possible" course of action will also make us grow in love. As we carry out all our duties, we will serve God while respecting Caesar. In pronouncing the distinction between the two realms of God and Caesar, Jesus is not separating the two authorities: Caesar's realm is never independent of God's. Caesar must submit to God. Politics is not exempt from moral laws, any more than it can ignore God's rights. If it did, obedience to God would take precedence over obedience to civil law. The Christians of the first centuries would suffer torture and death rather than sacrifice before the bust of emperors. On the other hand, they would pay taxes and duties, and when the authorities were at God's service for good, they would obey them.

The general rule stated by Jesus about Caesar applies to all circumstances in which our conscience is engaged. It applies to the affairs of the city and those of our profession, economic problems and social issues. Christians do not work out their salvation in the abstract. Rather, we work out our salvation in the reality of our daily occupations and duties of state. It is in the complexity of our daily tasks and worries that we must seek and follow God's will.

It is as Christians, with minds nourished by the Gospel and hearts overflowing with love for our brothers and sisters, that we must consider the everyday problems of our world: teaching and educating young people, slums, alcoholism, public morality, the status of work, unemployment, sickness, old age, and so much more. Under no circumstances must Christians desert their earthly function and their duty. Christians must render to Caesar what is Caesar's, though we do so by rendering to God the obedience owed to God.

In truth, our work is never finished, for we will never reach the point of perfect love. But it is precisely this continual charity that brings us closer to the Parousia. Faced with the possibility of unlimited progress, we would be understandably worried if we were left all alone to achieve it. But our Savior is with us. He himself will soon gather our modest efforts and join them to his sacrifice. In our name, he will render to God what is God's. We can rely on him who began the work of our sanctification to bring it to a successful conclusion. God himself will finish the job.

14

The Church Triumphant

> We are more than conquerors through him who loved us.
>
> —Romans 8:37

Under the Emperor Domitian's persecution, the apostle St. John was condemned to hard labor on the island of Patmos and kept from celebrating the holy mysteries with his brothers each week. But one Sunday he was granted a marvelous compensation. Delighted and ecstatic, he watched the heavenly liturgy unfold, with all the inhabitants of heaven taking part. How many of them are there? The seer tries to count them but gives up. Behind the righteous of Israel, he contemplates "a great multitude which no man could number, from every nation, from all tribes and peoples and tongues" (Rv 7:9).

Let's not expect to know in this life what happens behind the veil God lifted for John. The apostle has said enough for the Church to authorize the celebration of countless souls admitted to the vision of God. Alongside those made illustrious by martyrdom or heroic virtues, many others have entered whose memory is lost on earth. Among those unknown people God recognized as his own, some are linked to you by ties of blood or affection. When their parents' turn comes to render an account to God, a voice will plead for them in the eternal court: "Lord, they have given you a chosen one!" Won't the tenderness of the heavenly Father want to reunite these fathers and mothers with their children?

For the first two centuries, Christian devotion did not move far past the central figure of Jesus Christ. From the second century onwards, it became customary to pay homage to the martyrs on the anniversary of their death by celebrating the Eucharist at their tombs. In time, this cult of the martyrs, which was purely local, merged with the cult of the Savior, the martyr par excellence. The martyrs, his witnesses and imitators, "completed" the savior's sufferings, to use the language of St. Paul (Col 1:24). But because custom limited a martyr's honors to the burial place, the idea arose of venerating the memory of all martyrs. Subsequently, the devotion became a celebration of all saints.

This is the origin of the feast of All Saints. It originated in fourth-century Syria, and was celebrated during the Easter season in connection to the victory of the Risen Christ. The feast earns its name. It honors all God's children whom the redemption sanctified. It is the feast of the Church already triumphant, vanguards of the elect who will escort the Lord on the day of his coming.

Don't forget that the happiness of heaven is a collective happiness. Of heaven, as of hell, Our Lord spoke above all in images. How else could he have described to us an entirely spiritual world whose reality eludes our human imagination? The Master used images familiar to Jewish piety. In the Gospel, heaven is a feast, a wedding feast, a kingdom. It's the collective joy of all children personally loved together by their Father. All are seated at the same table, though in different places; all surround the King, though staggered around the same throne. Jesus told us, and this time in plain words: "In my Father's house are many rooms" (Jn 14:2).

Inside Heaven

"Many rooms" suggest that heaven involves a certain diversity. According to St. Augustine, the great number of abodes means that rewards vary by merits, but all within the same blessed eternity. In the Father's one house, all share in Christ's triumph, in proportion to their states of service. Is it not right that the most valiant should be more closely associated with the Head's victory? Hence it follows that the glory and felicity of the saints are both unequal and common.

Equality will no more reign in heaven than on earth, because the law of divine works is not equality, but *equity*. God gives each of his children the right gifts for the function he assigns them. This inequality in life is further emphasized by the fact that the external conditions of success are not identical for all. This inequality is mirrored in heaven, as the elect, having received unequal graces, have responded with unequal fidelity and generosity. The reward, to be fair, must be unequal between a Christian who has preserved his baptismal innocence and another who has returned to grace after years of indifference or sin, or between one who makes up for a few errors by lavishly giving their efforts in the service of Christ and another who has done neither great good nor great evil. The reward, if it is to be fair, must be unequal.

This inequality does not sadden the saints. They all contemplate the glory of the Blessed Virgin, far superior to their own: The sight provokes their admiration, and they rejoice in the honor Mary's holiness bestows on God. Each person's happiness makes the others happier. No one celebrates his or her own victory, but only the victory of the Leader. Everyone sees God, everyone possesses God, everyone's capacity for love is fully satisfied.

Heavenly Dwellers

However, all the saints are still alike in that, sooner or later, they followed the only road that leads to heaven: that of the eight beatitudes. Some accepted poverty, while others sought it out, but all shook off the tyranny of money. And because they were not slaves to Mammon, they were able to resist the bite of pride. They all entered heaven through the only door that gives access, the low and narrow door of humility. There is no place for the humble in hell. They are all in heaven. Mary, Queen of Heaven, was the humblest of the Lord's servants. The vision of God allows only those closed off to duplicity. The covetous, the liars, the deceivers, the seducers, the thieves, the murderers, and the blasphemers cannot contemplate the divine light. But all honest and delicate consciences, upright characters and pure hearts, are promised bliss.

The saints repented but did not despair. They continued to love and seek the good, though they accomplished it with great difficulty. Even for those who came later to thirst for God, they were able to learn in purgatory the joys of loving him. A last sigh can save a soul, if it's a sigh of love. And what is an act of contrition, if not a desire for holiness? Yet God would not grant sinners the grace of final conversion unless they had done some good during their lives. And the others, who lived in a state of grace, showed their obedience to God by devoting themselves to their brethren. They were gentle and compassionate to the suffering, forgetful of insults, and peacemakers among their fellows. Our little good deeds, the kind about which we say: “It’s only natural,” and then forget—above all those for which we have never been thanked—that’s what God will remember. It was not out of vanity or self-interest that we did these acts. Jesus will tell us that it was for him that we did them. Virtue that ignores itself is the way to heaven.

But the path of virtue is marked by suffering. St. John shows us the Lord wiping away the tears of his chosen ones (Rv 21:4). All the saints have wept here on earth: It’s the law of ascension. Tears are like the ballast with which the soul lifts itself up. Happy tears are those brought on by the pain of sin. Even more sanctifying are the healing tears shed by physical suffering or heartbreak.

There is, however, a nobler trial and more meritorious pain, that of the disciples of Jesus who endure persecution “for righteousness’ sake” (Mt 5:10). Happy are those who do not resign themselves to the pressure of violence, but fight against the injustice of the strongest. Happy are those who lead the fight against the social plagues that infect humanity. Happy are those wounded defending the rights of the weak and lost noble causes. Happy are those who die to bear witness to the truth! "Theirs is the kingdom of heaven!" (Mt 5:12). Still, it is not only the exceptional who reach heaven. God welcomes all his servants who show themselves faithful in the smallest things, who perform the ordinary actions of life with great love and courage.

15

Purgatory

And him who comes to me I will not cast out.

—John 6:37

"Remember also, Lord, your servants . . . who have gone before us with the sign of faith and rest in the sleep of peace."[1] With these words, the priest prays for the dead of the Church. I don't know how long it will be, but one day my baptismal name too will be silently pronounced at this august moment in the liturgy.

Firmly attached to the Church, having begged the Lord to forgive me my faults, I will have fallen asleep in the sleep of peace, among "all who sleep in Christ."[2] Will my eyes reopen and be able to withstand the purity of the Father's brilliance? Or will that brilliance cast a merciless light on what I did not have the courage or the time to purify?

---

1. *Daily Roman Missal*, 3rd ed. (Midwest Theological Forum, 2019), "Eucharistic Prayer I," p. 799.

2. *Daily Roman Missal*, p. 799.

The doctrine of purgatory can reassure us in our weakness. Many of the unfortunates who separated from Holy Mother Church abandoned these riches of the old Christian heritage and retained only that which increases our fear: predestination and hell without mercy. Certainly, at the time of the Reformation, disgusting abuses could explain a great deal of anger. Now, in a relaxed, sanitized atmosphere, we find it hard to understand the criticisms levelled at *true* Catholic doctrine on purgatory. As for us, let's try to get to know it well so that we can make use of the lessons it offers.

When the councils of Florence and Trent, in the fifteenth and sixteenth centuries, defined the dogma of purgatory, it became clear that many theological opinions previously held in the Latin Church went far beyond the scope of the Faith. The authority of the infallible magisterium has solemnly affirmed: first, the existence of purifying punishments beyond this life, and second, the usefulness of the prayers for the faithful departed.

Some object that this dogma is not explicitly stated in Scripture. This criticism would only be valid if the books of the New Testament were written to codify the whole doctrine of Jesus Christ, with Tradition only having to comment on this written text. Such a view is historically false. The doctrine of Jesus was preached before the appearance of the writings, which captured only a part of the primitive oral tradition—and, as far as the epistles are concerned, only occasionally. Far from Tradition being the development of a complete and definitive text, Scripture contains only fragments of traditional teaching. This is why the Catholic Church does not base its faith solely on the Holy Books, but on the whole of apostolic preaching, as heard by the first Christian generation and passed on to the next.

The practice of praying for the dead was already in force among the Jews before the coming of Our Lord (see 2 Mc 12:39–46), and not a word of Jesus gives us reason to believe that he condemned this practice. To the contrary, several passages in the Gospel support it.

Temporal and Eternal Punishment

In several parables, the Savior exhorts his disciples to be ready for the day of his return, "for the Son of man is coming at an hour you do not expect" (Mt 24:44). One of these parables is that of the "guilty servants." It follows the story of the steward who, instead of carrying out his duties, quarreled with the servants and got drunk. His master, appearing unexpectedly, chased him away and condemned him to share the fate of "the hypocrites" (Mt 24:51). This steward is undoubtedly an image of the damned. But in Luke 12:47, two servants both neglected their work. The first knew perfectly well his master's will and ignored it, for which he will be severely punished. The second did not know well his master's will, since he was unaware of his duties, and he will receive a lesser punishment. Either these words mean nothing, or they imply that the punishments after death are not uniform, but proportionate to our responsibility, and less severe than eternal punishment.

Another example sheds further light. Jesus condemns the Pharisees who accused him of exorcising demoniacs with the power of Satan. While other sins can be forgiven, "whoever speaks against the Holy Spirit will not be forgiven" (Mt 12:32). The Lord specifies that God will forgive any sin for those who repent. Willful blindness (sin against the light), however, can never be forgiven, because it rejects all repentance.

However, the most solid foundation for the existence of purgatory is to be found in Tradition. From her very beginnings, the Church has prayed for the faithful departed. This prayer would be pointless if there were no intermediate state between damnation and the beatific vision. Since the Church has always prayed for the departed, it has always believed that the fate of its children may not be definitively determined at the hour of their demise.

Evidence for this practice dates to the first century Christian cemeteries in Rome. Frescoes found on the catacomb walls depict Daniel in the lion's den, the Hebrews crossing the Red Sea, David overcoming Goliath, or the three children in the furnace—all biblical scenes suggesting that the victory of the deceased has not yet been won. Two tombs from the middle of the second century bear similarly suggestive inscriptions. The first reads *Orare pro me, peccatore* (Pray for me, sinner). On the other: *Qui legis, ora pro eo* (Reader, pray for him).

The early Church Fathers upheld the practice of praying for the dead, whether it was Tertullian describing offerings for the deceased, or the canon of the Mass which prays for "refreshment, light, and peace" for the faithful departed.[3] St. Cyprian explains that in the other world, souls are subjected to different treatments:

> It is one thing to stand for pardon; another to arrive at glory. It is one thing for one put in prison to not come out of there until one has "paid the last penny"; another thing to receive immediately the reward of faith and virtue.[4]

---

3. *Daily Roman Missal*, p. 799.

4. Cyprian, *The Fathers of the Church: St. Cyprian Letters 1–81*, trans. Sr. Rose Bernard Donna, (Catholic University of America Press, 1981), p. 146.

From the fourth century onwards, the number of testimonies is endless. Besides these, we have no other certainty about purgatory. The believer is free to accept or reject opinions foreign to the primitive tradition, and free to think that certain questions raised by human curiosity are perfectly insoluble.

Such is the case with the duration of purgatory. Our way of measuring time has no meaning outside our solar system. The very notion of duration is relative. We know, for example, that in the dream state, a long and complicated dream lasts only one or two seconds. St. Peter says: "With the Lord one day is as a thousand years, and a thousand years as one day" (2 Pt 3:8). God's measures are not ours.

Purgative "fire" is a belief based on an inaccurate interpretation of a text by St. Paul and professed only in the Latin Church. The Greek Church never spoke of purgative fires, and the Council of Florence did not reproach them for this. As purifying atonement is inflicted only on souls, it is difficult to conceive what "sensitive" suffering is, when the sense organs and nerve centers have disappeared. At least, we have no experience of it. So, it is rather rash to claim to compare the sufferings of purgatory with those of earth.

St. Thomas declares, after St. Augustine, that the lightest of purgatorial pains exceeds all the pains that men feel in this world. St. Bonaventure and Suarez, on the contrary, believe that purgatory has lesser punishments than the most severe on earth. The question ceases to be unanswerable if we hold to the primitive tradition, preserved by the Eastern Fathers, who speak of the shame, affliction, sorrow, and pain of souls in purgatory. In this respect, it is not difficult to argue that the sufferings of these souls exceed those we experience now. And since present trials are the providential means by which we expiate our sins here below, it would be hard to understand why the punishments of purgatory should be less severe than those of this life.

The soul that leaves this world in a state of grace recognizes that God is its only good. It reaches out to him with all its strength. But if the awareness of its unworthiness prevents it from throwing itself into his arms, it feels an infinitely painful heartbreak. Let's not forget that some souls in purgatory were only delivered from sin at the last minute of their lives. All of them, however, see that God is not satisfied (this term is both theological and psychological). Knowing more clearly the goodness of God, they discover the full gravity of sin, they feel an insurmountable horror of it, and they want to share in the sufferings by which our Savior redeemed the sinful world.

Their unfortunate fate afflicts them less than the feeling of having responded so badly to God's love.

They cannot excuse themselves for having neglected or treated so badly a lovable God. Yet, another aspect of purgatory cannot be ignored. We are still in the realm of free beliefs: This one, however, is based on the authority of St. Catherine of Genoa and St. Francis de Sales:[5] If the deceased souls are in the state of grace, then they are assured of attaining the beatific vision, and completely abandoned to God's will. Whatever their pains, in their apprenticeship to heaven they doubtless experience incredible joys that help them to bear their sorrows.

Given that the sufferings in purgatory are more severe than those on earth, it is only natural that the joys in purgatory should also outweigh our own, both in quality and intensity. Souls in purgatory are happy because they are sure of being saved. (On earth, we hope for salvation through God's mercy; in purgatory, hope has given way to certainty.) Their happiness is no less for being unable to sin. And they love God above all else, without any selfish motives. They are content with God. They find it just, good, and necessary that heaven cannot welcome them until they have erased the last vestiges of sin.

---

5. See Catherine of Genoa's *Treatise on Purgatory* and Frederick W. Faber's *All for Jesus*, particularly chapter nine.

Anyone who is surprised that souls awaiting heaven can experience pain and joy at the same time should recall the amazing story of the good thief. This sinner endured atrocious tortures on his cross, but he suffered alongside Jesus, as if enveloped in the Savior's holy patience. When he heard his divine companion say: "Today you will be with me in Paradise," his suffering remained just as acute, but he also tasted the endless happiness that awaited him (Lk 23:43). As we can see, the Catholic doctrine of purgatory is equally in line with God's justice and mercy, and in no way offends the demands of reason. The Lord Jesus did not declare in vain that "when I go to prepare a place for you, I will come again and will take you to myself" (Jn 14:3).

Strengthened by this hope, we remember our deceased with great gentleness. Just as we assisted them during their last illness, we continue to watch over them, but now we are certain that their sufferings are truly alleviated by our prayers. Let us pray for all the faithful departed. The Lord asks us to practice charity: "I was in prison and you came to me" (Mt 26:36). If our suffrages and feeble merits help the souls in purgatory to glorify God in heaven sooner, we will have our share in their tribute to God's glory.

16

From the Churches on Earth to the Church in Heaven

The dwelling of God is with men.
—Revelations 21:3

In November, Catholics celebrate the anniversaries of the great Roman basilicas: St. John Lateran and Sts. Peter and Paul. The same sentiment of these celebrations can be found in the Book of Genesis: "How awesome is this place! This is none other than the house of God, and this is the gate of heaven" (Gen 28:17). This is what Jacob said when he awoke from a dream in which he had seen the mysterious ladder linking the ground to heaven, and through which the angels of God ascended and descended. "Surely the Lord is in this place," cried the patriarch, "and I did not know it" (Gen 28:16). Immediately, taking the stone that had served as his bedside table, he anointed it with oil and made it an altar to the glory of the Lord.

So it is with our churches. Consecrated to God, they unite earth with heaven. As if by an invisible ladder, heavenly messengers bring our prayers to God and bring us back his graces. Yet this ladder lacks the middle rung, indeed an essential rung, which is the Church.

To get a better understanding, imagine a play that takes place simultaneously on three stages. This is exactly the liturgical drama that takes place within our churches. We are faced with three planes: the material plane, the spiritual plane, and the eternal plane, brought together in a way described by the Apostle John in Revelation: *Ecce tabernaculum Dei cum hominibus*, "Behold, the dwelling of God is with men" (Rv 21:3). In a single glance we see three dwellings of God in one: first, *our material churches*, which are the figure of the Church; second, *the spiritual society* instituted by Jesus, which is itself the type of the third reality: *the future City of God,* to which the children of God will be admitted after the general resurrection.

Churches Are the Houses of God

The celebration of the liturgy awakens in us a respectful love for our churches, built by human hands for the celebration of divine worship. There are still a few who find fault, not just with the "luxury" of churches, but with their very existence: "How can we confine the infinite God who is everywhere to a building, when we can adore him in nature and hear him in our conscience?" I want to believe that these people really don't need a church to pray. God *is* everywhere, but in our feverish existence, we risk finding him nowhere for lack of silence. Zacchaeus was a rich tax collector who hoped to see Jesus by climbing a sycamore tree. Zacchaeus certainly saw him, but if the Lord hadn't said to him: "I must stay with you today," would this sinner have heard what the Savior said to the depths of his heart? That encounter saved Zacchaeus and his whole family.[1]

True, God sometimes speaks to us in the hubbub of the street, more clearly and more deeply than in the distractions of our church prayers. Yet, when we seek him, when we need to hear him, it's not in the tumult that we find him. Today, very few people can easily "close their bedroom door and pray to the Father in secret."[2] We're more likely to find him in our churches. And isn't it right that there is a special building among the houses of a town or village to remind everyone of God's presence amid humanity?

---

1. "And when Jesus came to the place, he looked up and said to him, 'Zacchaeus, make haste and come down; for I must stay at your house today.'" (Lk 19:5)

2. "But when you pray, go into your room and shut the door and pray to your Father who is in secret; and your Father who sees in secret will reward you." (Mt 6:6)

As soon as we enter our churches, even before greeting the tabernacle and the cross, we sense an atmosphere of prayer. So many others have come before us to express their desires, their distresses, their regrets! However, the church is only secondarily the house of the Christian people. First and foremost, churches are the house of God. We don't receive God into our homes; God receives us into his. Let us always enter with respect.

The very styles of our churches invite our respectful prayer. Our churches are the ark where God shelters us from the flood of our sins: hence their frequent shape as an inverted ship (nave). It's in our churches that God accepts the merits of Jesus Christ: hence their habitual cross shape. We are here in the antechamber that opens into heaven: hence the high vaults in our churches.

In the Father's house, however, children are not strangers. In this sense alone, the Father's house is also ours, but it is ours in a communal capacity: "My house shall be a house of prayer" (Lk 19:46). Open to all who wish to gather, by its very nature it is not a place for private prayer. Its proper purpose is public, collective prayer: It's where the *ecclesia* gathers.

The Spiritual Church Is the Body of Christ

On the stage where the "play" of the liturgy takes place, let's now examine the second stage, where the spiritual Church appears, of which the material edifice was the figure. We won't quibble with the passers-by of good will who declare with conviction that they never pray as well as outside of services, when there are very few people in church. Let them at least have eyes to see! What is the significance of the pulpit, the baptismal fount, the altar at the back, or the confessional on the side? Everything here speaks to us of the Church of Jesus Christ, whose head resides in Rome, as recalled by the statue of St. Peter holding in his hand the keys of the kingdom. Within the walls of the material church, Holy Mother Church sanctifies her children.

From this pulpit, we learn the truth that frees us from all our soul's questions. Tossed about by the opposing currents of philosophical systems that battle for minds, we find intellectual peace only in our Church. She alone has the audacity to denounce error. Her doctrine is that of Christ who "sent" her, and it is also his law. Her wisdom is equally far removed from a thoughtless stoicism or lukewarm complacency.

The Church brings us to life in Jesus Christ through baptism. Better still, it joins us into him, so we become his members. Often, a cross dominates the altar in our churches. Here, the Church proclaims the redemptive death of our Savior: Through this death, we can offer Christ to God in atonement for our sins. In the past, the cross did not bear the image of the Crucified One: no representation was allowed to distract the mind from the true Body of Christ present in the Mass. From this body, each of us is nourished, so that divine life may develop in our souls. Do we tremble at not being pure enough to receive it?

From the house of stone, we move on to the image of a *living house,* whose Christians are so many stones cemented together to gradually build the Temple of God on earth. This image comes from St. Peter. "Come to him," he writes, "like living stones be yourselves built into a spiritual house, to be a holy priesthood, to offer spiritual sacrifices acceptable to God through Jesus Christ" (1 Pt 2:4–5). This second image is superimposed on the first, through it the house now signifies the entire family. The Church, the society of Christians, is *the family* of God's children. On the lower (material) level, to build a new church is to build a new family home, destined for a certain portion of the Christian people. Transpose this motif to the second (spiritual) plane and we see that the dedication of a church evokes the day on which the Christian family was founded. In mystical language, the dedication of a church is *the wedding day* on which Jesus Christ married the Church.

The Heavenly Church

The heavenly Church, the glorious fulfillment of the earthly Church, shows us what God's people will become. This Church, whose jeweled gates are open to all mortals who shared Christ's sorrows for his sake, has its foundations on earth. The apostles and prophets form its foundations, and all Christians are "living stones," cut and polished by the chisel and hammer of the Divine Worker, whose blows have given them the form of holiness. The three metaphorical motifs outlined above reappear in light of the future city. This final Church will be God's permanent dwelling place among humans, "that God may be everything to everyone" (1 Cor 15:28).

Far more than our material churches, even more than the spiritual Church here below, the eternal Church will be God's *house*, the Father's house of many dwellings. "He will dwell with them, and they shall be his people, and God himself will be with them" (Rv 21:3).

The mystical marriage contracted silently on the day of the Incarnation in the womb of the Blessed Virgin Mary between the Son of God and humanity will, on the day of the Parousia, be celebrated with splendor. The Bride—the Church, our mother—whom he has raised from an abyss of misery will, on that day, be the most beautiful of queens. She will descend beside her Bridegroom onto a renewed earth, the final kingdom of God.

Last but not least, the theme of the *divine family* is fully realized on the eternal plane. It is here, in our stone churches, that we have been recreated as children of God by the Holy Spirit acting through the sacraments of the Church. This inner regeneration has begun and is developing here below. In the Church on earth, as St. Paul writes, "we all, with unveiled face, beholding the glory of the Lord, are being changed into his likeness from one degree of glory to another; for this comes from the Lord who is the Spirit" (2 Cor 3:18).

But later, regenerated humanity will have reached "the stature of the fulness of Christ" (Eph 4:13). The new man will have as his habitat a new world, of which the epistle gives us the promise:

> "Death shall be no more, neither shall there be mourning nor crying nor pain any more, for the former things have passed away." And he who sat upon the throne said, "Behold, I make all things new." (Rv 21:4–5)

St. Paul underlines the continuity that exists for the Christian between heaven and earth: between the cries of the little child being baptized, and the joy of the chosen one in a transformed world. Our early lives are a continuous journey through our earthly churches into the perpetual communion of heaven. They reveal the value we should attach to everything that bears the name of Church, "God's dwelling among men."

17

The Sleep of Death

The girl is not dead but sleeping.

—Matthew 9:24

The ninth chapter of Matthew's Gospel foreshadows the approaching end times, or at least that is the interpretation given to it by St. Jerome.[1] The daughter of Jairus, he said, is allegorically the Jewish nation, and the woman with the hemorrhage represents the Gentiles. The Lord was delayed from healing the daughter of Jairus by the woman with the hemorrhage. Meanwhile, the little Jewish girl was dying, but Jesus gave her back her life. Today, in God's providence, the Jewish people seem to be neglected at present like the little girl, while the Gentiles receive the Gospel. Before the world ends, however, Israel will be converted. St. Paul did not want us to ignore this mystery: "A hardening has come upon part of Israel, until the full number of the Gentiles come in, and so all Israel will be saved" (Rom 11:25–26).

---

1. Jerome, *The Homilies of Saint Jerome*, vol.1 (Catholic University of America Press, 1964), p. 241.

For us who will die before the world's end, what will it be like to leave this earth? Our Lord answered this question by calling back to life a child who had just died. When the synagogue ruler presents himself to Jesus, his child is still alive, which makes his request more urgent. He falls at the Savior's feet and begs him: "My little daughter is at the point of death. Come and lay your hands on her, so that she may be made well, and live" (Mk 5:23).

How could the Master resist this request? A twelve-year-old girl is not supposed to die. The poor father is in despair. His little girl, this exquisite being of purity and charm, is passing from this world! St. Mark writes: "He [Jesus] went with him. And a great crowd followed him and thronged about him" (5:24). It was at this point that the Gentile woman intervened. No sooner had the sick woman been cured, though, than Jairus's neighbors come and say, "Your daughter is dead. Why trouble the Teacher any further?" Immediately our merciful Jesus turns to the synagogue ruler: "Do not fear, only believe" (Mk 5:35-36). When the Savior enters the home, the customary rites are already taking place. The flute players have begun to play their mournful dirges, and mourners lament the child's death.

The pity in Jesus's eyes gives way to authority: "Why do you make a tumult and weep? The child is not dead but sleeping." The public's reaction was instantaneous. "They laughed at him" (Mk 5:39-40). They knew she was dead. When you're dead, there's no hope. Jesus kicks everyone out.

Accompanied by the mother and father, their relatives, and the three great apostles, he enters the room where the dead girl lays on her bed. Her parents, their eyes fixed with pain and a hope they dare not define, hold their breath. Jesus takes the child's hand. "'*Tal'itha cu'mi*'; which means, 'Little girl, I say to you, arise.'" Jesus used the very words her mother spoke to her every morning when she woke up. "And immediately the girl got up and walked" (Mk 5:41–42). Jesus, who kept his presence of mind amidst the general commotion, ordered that she be given something to eat.

It's hard to remain unmoved by the natural tone of this story, in which no attempt is made to achieve a desired effect. Everything just happens. It's so simple to die! It's just as simple to rise again. Death doesn't end anything, it's a sleep from which Jesus will awaken us.

The Three Resurrections in the Gospels

The Gospel contains three accounts of resurrections. Those who were the object of these miracles gained nothing more than having to continue their earthly ordeal, and they had to descend a second time into the darkness of death. In bringing them back to life, the Savior thought of those who mourned them. In all three cases, he gave in to a spontaneous movement of compassion: before the grief of the widow of Naim, Jairus, and the sisters of Lazarus.

How grateful we are for Jesus's sympathy. He could have merely consoled the unfortunate parents by saying: "You will see your loved ones in heaven," but he knows the temptations suffering people face: *Will we ever see them again? Do we still live when the heart has stopped beating?* The Master was eager to build up their hopes and ours. Martha of Bethany, like us, clung to her faith. "I know," she said, "that he will rise again in the resurrection at the last day" (Jn 11:24). Jesus wants her hope to be a certainty. Her brother had not ceased to live, even though he was locked in the tomb with his hands and feet bound in bandages: "'Lazarus, come out.' The dead man came out" (Jn 11:43–44).

Note that none of the three resurrected in the Gospel, nor Tabitha or Eutychus, respectively called back to life by St. Peter and St. Paul, were "resurrected" in the literal sense of the word, as we will be one day. They did not enter a new life, endowed with a transformed body. Would they have returned to us if they had seen God face to face? They only resumed their former lives. They had not ceased to live. On hearing the news of Lazarus's death, the Savior had said, "Our friend Lazarus has fallen asleep, but I go to awake him" (Jn 11:11). Lazarus was asleep, just as Jairus's daughter was only asleep. There's no mistaking the meaning of his statement; those who mock him will be sorry for their confusion. One word from Jesus and you can be sure that the deceased still live. Death does not take away life; it is sleep.

Christian Views of Death

People can sometimes make fun of Christians for seeing the cemetery as something more than an ossuary, or bone yard. For us, the cemetery has retained its original meaning: *κοιμητήριον*, the "dormitory" where our departed rest in Christ awaiting the blessed resurrection.

"The child is not dead but sleeping" (Mk 5:39). The liturgy adapts Christ's words in the preface of Masses for the dead: "For your faithful, Lord, life is changed, not ended."[2] For the convenience of language, we distinguish between the present life and the future life. In reality, God will not give us another life after the first has passed away. He has *given* us life, a single life, which is to blossom into eternity.

"God did not make death" (Wis 1:13), but by rebelling against its Author, humankind has condemned

2. *Daily Roman Missal*, p. 763.

itself to suffer the fate of creatures made solely for the earth. Despite this, humans do not feel destined to die. Not only does the obscure instinct for self-preservation, which we share with all animals, drive us, like them, to flee death, but a deeper law of our nature prevents us from considering death as the end of our efforts and life's crowning achievements. We are not made to die. Death is a break, slow or sudden, that strikes us while we are still capable of loving, producing, and living. St. Paul writes: "Though our outer nature is wasting away, our inner nature is being renewed every day" (2 Cor 4:16).

The material elements of our body are constantly disappearing and being reborn. Yet, beneath this whirlwind of matter, our true personality remains the same, partially freed from space and time. We live in a spiritual world made up of memories, admirations, enthusiasms, repentances, and sorrows. This world cannot be reduced to our corporeal organism. We've known unforgettable moments, such as the joy of knowing and understanding, or the strength to love to the point of renunciation, or the hour of great sacrifice. But isn't pronouncing God's blessed name alone enough to convince us that in the immensity of the universe we count in his eyes? God would be inconceivable to us if, having allowed us to know and love him, at the very moment when our arms are about to embrace him, he were to shrink back and leave us with the bitterness of a chimera. The hour of our departure is, in the divine plan, the hour when he whom we called "Father" will prove to us his love.

Would we say that death does not exist for the Christian? Alas! there is a terrible death that we must dread. It is the work of sin, which not in vain bears the name "mortal," for it detaches us from God and isolates us in creation, without support or hope. This is the "second death" of which St. John speaks:

> But as for the cowardly, the faithless, the polluted, as for murderers, fornicators, sorcerers, idolaters, and all liars, their lot shall be in the lake that burns with fire and brimstone, which is the second death. (Rv 21:8)

The Christian who rejects God has definitively lost divine life forever. If this unfortunate person does not repent, they are already a corpse, but the faithful Christian "will never see death" (Jn 8:51). When we complete this time of trial, our life will change. It cannot be taken away from us, for the germ of divine life that we received in baptism, and which the Eucharist made grow, cannot be touched by physical death. The Christian united with God enters fullness of life.

So, death will be for us the passage to definitive life: a passing, a Passover. But when this passage opens up before us, will we have to suppress a shudder? The last detaching may be costly. How can we not be apprehensive about such a serious act, of which we have no prior experience? All this is normal, since death is the punishment for sin. It is therefore appropriate that it should include a painful element for us. But this pain will win us great merit.

Preparing for Death

"Behold," says the Lord, "I stand at the door and knock; if anyone hears my voice and opens the door, I will come in to him and eat with him, and he with me" (Rv 3:20). Jesus speaks of the hour of our death, for the Voice continues, "He who conquers, I will grant him to sit with me on my throne" (Rv 3:21). The Lord will surely come unexpectedly, like an unannounced thief; but instead of breaking down the door, he will knock and, with the delicacy of a friend, ask us to open up to him. He gives us the chance to offer him what he could take anytime. In our last moments, we can make a sacrifice, a holy offering.

The sacrifice of humility: *Lord, you are the master of our days. You have chosen this hour, I adore your plans.*

The sacrifice of repentance: *Accept my suffering in reparation for my faults. I renounce the goods that have sometimes turned me away from you.*

The sacrifice of obedience: *I have haggled over it so many times. Today, Lord, I no longer argue. Thy will be done! From now on, I will no longer disobey you.*

Finally, a sacrifice of love: *I haven't loved you enough! Let my last sigh be a sigh of love, the mite of the widow who gave all she had. All I have left is my poor heart, take it.*

But why leave our salvation for the last days? Let us mortify now what death will destroy forever: our pride, our greed, our sensuality. The offering that will precede the great sleep, let us present it every evening, before we fall asleep, looking at Jesus dying on his cross.

This look at the cross will remind us that the agony and death of all Christians have already been offered to God by our Savior. In none of the mysteries of his life was Jesus Christ alone. All the members of the body of which he is the Head were with him: Our old man, our sinful self, was therefore bound up with him on the cross.

If every evening, I consciously unite my death with that of Jesus, then, when I breathe my last, I will be both victim and oblation with Jesus already. I will offer with Jesus, to his Father, my death with Christ's. Now, this offering of my death will already have been accepted by the Father, just as when the Savior uttered his great cry: "It is finished!" (Jn 19:30). All that remains for us then is to bow our head, like our divine Model, and say after him: "Father, into your hands I commend my spirit" (Lk 23:46).

God has permitted that the very moment of death should not be terrible. The dying person's numbed sensibility no longer perceives pain; the conscience darkens as if to veil the beings and things from which the soul is separating; no anxiety can be read on the face. A loved one begins the agonizing prayer: "Go forth, Christian soul, from this world in the name of God the almighty Father, who created you, in the name of Jesus Christ. . . ."[3] Does the dying one even hear the refrain of the litanies? Wrapped in a shroud of silence, the soul receives the final graces that God has attached to the sleep of death. The gentle Virgin Mary is present, right at the hour when she was so often asked to assist the departing. The Christian is not dead: But their eyes must be closed. They have fallen asleep in *Life*.

---

3. *Catechism of the Catholic Church*, 2nd ed. (Libreria Editrice Vaticana–United States Conference of Catholic Bishops, 2000), no. 1020.

18

The Transformed Body

> The Lord Jesus Christ . . . will change our lowly body to be like his glorious body.
>
> —Philippians 3:20

Now we return from the sleep of death to the conditions of our awakening. A reminder of this transformation comes in the words of the Nicene Creed: "I look forward to the resurrection of the dead." The Apostles' Creed formula, "I believe in . . . the resurrection of the body" means that the body will participate in our glorious state.

However, some of the faithful are a little embarrassed by this dogma. They would be content, they say, with the immortality of the soul, which seems easier to accept. They hardly see what a spiritual body can add. But ask yourself, are we mere philosophers or are we Christians? In the latter case, let's not use a flawed method. As Christians, we hold to be true what the Son of God certainly taught. Since Jesus declared that he will resurrect us on the last day, we should verify what this means and give it our faith. Afterwards—but only afterwards—let us listen to the questions of our reason. Then we'll see that they can't shake our belief, which strengthens the more we deepen it.

We all remember Jesus's words. He declares not just the immortality of the body, but the immortality of the whole person. When he brought Lazarus out of the tomb, he spoke of the resurrection of the just. He himself will be the author of these resurrections, for they are the consequence of his life in us, a life to which we have access through faith.

Since Plato, belief in the soul's immortality was familiar to the Greek philosophical world. Plato believed that the body, the material shell of the soul, deserved only the corruption of the grave. In Athens, when St. Paul alluded to the resurrection of the dead, he had to stop his speech because of the mocking laughter from the Areopagus. In his letters to Corinth, Paul warns that his teaching is the same as all the apostles (1 Cor 15:20–27). His thesis can be summed up as follows: Irrefutable testimonies establish that Christ is risen, and Jesus's own resurrection is the cause and model of our own. If Jesus were the only one to have escaped death, it would not have been defeated. If death continued to have the upper hand, then the world of sin would not be destroyed. Like our Head, we will go down to the tomb, but death can no longer hold us there: Jesus has torn away its sting.

Let's shake off the bad dreams that assail us on sad evenings, when we wish we would sleep and never wake again. Jesus's resurrection not only authorizes us to hope that we will rise again, but also forbids us to suppose that we will not rise with him in our flesh. Humans are both body and soul: a soul, certainly, but living in a body, a body animated by a soul. At present, the body guarantees and protects our individuality. Why, in our future mode of existence, should it not also guarantee our personality? Will I admit that the immortality of the soul alone is a more impenetrable mystery to my feeble understanding than that of the resurrection of the flesh? What is the life of the soul separated from the body, and how does it retain its personal consciousness? We have no experience of this, and no analogy. Fortunately, the truth of religious dogmas is not based on our greater or lesser ability to explain them.

What could be more just, however, than the resurrection of the body! Our body has had a very large part in the conduct of our life. Is it not entitled to its share of reward, this body which has accomplished, by the sweat of its brow, the work that God commands us? This body which, yielding to the remorse of conscience, has shed tears of repentance? This body that stiffened under fatigue to allow our spirit to keep watch? This body capable of realizing the boldest conceptions of the artist's or craftsman's genius? Think of all that is contained in the expression of a look: Will there be nothing left of it? Will we be weaned forever from all the charm of the human voice? I know—Jesus said so—that after the resurrection, man and woman will love each other like angels: At least they will continue to love each other, and therefore to say so.

Body as Receptacle of Grace

But there's more. For us Christians, the body is the vehicle of the grace that transfigures our souls: It is the body that is moistened by the water of baptism and the oil of confirmation. St. Paul reminds us that the body is also the temple of the Holy Spirit (1 Cor 6:15–20). To appreciate the significance of this expression, it's worth placing it in context. "Your body is yours," claim pagans, ancient and modern, to justify their abuse of it. Such language would be blasphemy on Christian lips. We don't have the right to "profane" our bodies, because they don't belong to us. Our bodies belong to Christ, who bought them dearly enough. They belong to the Holy Spirit, who dwells in them as in his temple. By keeping our body chaste, we glorify God in it, and because we have left it to him, God will resurrect it.

Catholic teaching specifies that it is not the molecules of our body that will come back to life. Theologians call the principle that maintains the organism's identity "substance." Just as in the Eucharist we do not consume the molecules of Christ's body, but the *substance* of his body, so it is the substance of our body that will live again. To give us an idea, St. Paul uses a comparison drawn from the germination of plants. The seed buried in the earth begins by dying, but a force proceeds from it which organizes the surrounding matter and produces a plant quite different from the seed. Thus, writes the Apostle, "what is sown is perishable, what is raised is imperishable. It is sown in dishonor, it is raised in glory . . . It is sown a physical body, it is raised a spiritual body" (1 Cor 15:42–44).

How can we imagine our future body? The Lord will transform our body of misery into a body similar to his glorious body. On Easter evening, the body of Jesus passed through the walls (Jn 20). It was not bound by laws of earthly matter. If the risen body is a different material than any we now know, however, in its deepest reality it will still retain its identity. The apostles recognized the scars of the crucifixion on Our Lord's body.

The image we have of heaven is fatally flawed, and certainly sub-reality. Heaven is first and foremost life with God—and therefore a never-ending beatitude, because it is always new—but the resurrection of the body will increase our happiness. St. Thomas Aquinas teaches that, after the resurrection of the body, the beatitude of the soul itself will increase in scope and intensity. What's more, the blessed, having been given a glorious body, will not be fixed in an immobile ecstasy. Without leaving God, they will enjoy a fully free and active life. We can aid God's plan by living as citizens of heaven on earth. Let us offer God a body that is willing, supple, full of life, and able to carry out its work with zest. And, most importantly, let us also sanctify it by weaning it from all sin, through strict discipline.

19

The Age to Come

> But according to his promise, we wait for new heavens and a new earth in which righteousness dwells.
>
> —2 Peter 3:13

The final article of the Nicene Creed reads: "And I look forward to . . . the life of the world to come." The present world will undergo a sudden cataclysm. Our Lord depicted it using metaphors already employed by the prophets: The sun will be darkened, the moon will no longer give its brightness, the stars will fall from heaven, the powers of the heavens will be shaken, while, with the loud sound of the trumpet, the angels will gather the elect. Matthew 24 reminds us of the final meaning of earthly history, with its spectacular culmination into a history that will never end. A few preliminary explanations will help us understand this better.

The Two Eschatological Prophecies

Our Lord's eschatological[1] discourse comprises two prophecies: The first concerns the ruin of Jerusalem, the second the Parousia and the end of the world. The transition from one to the other, clearly marked in Luke 21:24, is less apparent in St. Matthew. It is easy to imagine that, at the end of the world, no one will think of taking his mantle from his home, and no escape will be possible. However, these indications are also perfectly suited to the days preceding the siege of Jerusalem (Mt 24:21). The Christians of the early Church carefully collected the two prophecies the Master made on the eve of his death. But in their reverent admiration for the Temple, it seemed impossible that after its destruction the world should continue to exist. And since their generation was to see this dreadful catastrophe, it would also see the end of the world: The two events would be concomitant. Quite naturally, the two distinct predictions, with similar themes, became one in their minds.

That's why Jesus's prophecy of destruction is placed after the announcement of the Parousia, which never fails to trouble some of the faithful every year. That this precision refers only to the ruin of Jerusalem can be seen

1. Concerning the end of the world.

two verses later. Jesus continues to speak of the Parousia, first in plain language, then in parables. In Matthew 24:36, the Master affirms that, "that day and that hour" are known only to the Father (see also Mark 13:32). How could he have contradicted himself by declaring that the same event would take place during the disciples' lifetime, while he himself was unaware of the day and hour? Clearly, the Father's secret concerns the time of Judgment, and what the generation listening to him will see is the destruction of the Temple.

Note the fact that the first three Gospels were written, known, and spread before the sack of Jerusalem by Titus's soldiers. Had they been written after the year AD 70—when the holy city was no more than a heap of ruins and the Parousia had not occurred—the evangelists would not have failed to dissociate the two prophecies; perhaps they would even have emphasized the fulfillment of the first. Nonetheless, the Holy Books continued to be copied without rectification. As they were, so they remain. The text was certainly written in the years before AD 70, and the little phrase "this generation will not pass away," which scandalizes the uninformed reader, dates the composition of the Gospels and attests that they were the work of Jesus's very first disciples (Mt 24:34).

Jesus announced the desolation of the holy place (this desecration took place in the year 68), and ends with the proclamation: "Heaven and earth will pass away, but my words will not pass away" (Mt 24:35). Wouldn't the lesson before us be just this? The Lord announced the first and last stages of Church history. The end of Judaism took place as he predicted; so will the final judgment. The destiny of the Christian people, the new people of God, is not left to chance. Both the development and the completion of its history will unfold according to divine plan. The Church will not be an establishment, but a movement.

During the first generation, the Church retained the imprint of the Judaism from which it had sprung, and recruited its first followers from the Jewish world. Under these conditions, Christianity was in great danger of becoming nothing more than the religion of one race. So God soon withdrew the support it needed for its beginnings. Jerusalem was overthrown, the Temple fell prey to the flames, and the ancient cult of Israel was abolished.

God's Plan for the Church

However, while the old Judaic tree is cut down, the Church has preserved all that was not to pass from the Old Covenant. A wider world, the Greco-Roman world, opened up before the preachers of the Gospel. It consisted of all countries subject to Rome, fringed by unexplored regions populated with barbarians. After two and a half centuries of persecution, Christianity managed to penetrate Roman civilization. Would the Church tie its fate to that of Rome, an aging society? The Church must not become established, but continue to conquer the earth. So, barbarians swept toward the Mediterranean. Rome was destroyed by Alaric as Jerusalem had been by Titus. The Roman Empire has passed away, but Jesus's words have not.

After the second framework cracked, the world to be evangelized expanded. God's people set off for a third stage, now spreading out among the barbarian peoples. Clovis and Charlemagne replaced Constantine. The Church converted Europe. Medieval Christianity came to rely on the dual support of the Holy Roman Empire and the Holy See, arbiter of nations. But would Christianity's spirit of conquest fade? Alas, the salt has diminished. New cracks are starting to show. Unprecedented tribulations are shattering medieval Christianity and tearing religious unity apart. Half of Europe broke with the papacy. Is the Christian people left to weep over ruins?

The Holy Spirit won't permit it, because the face of the earth has not yet been renewed. The medieval frameworks have collapsed under the pressure of a reborn paganism. The Church's accidental insertion into the temporal order, which is not its own, ended in a bitter failure, but from this horrible bankruptcy a new world has emerged, the *modern world.* The Gospel will go beyond the borders of Europe. Columbus discovered America, Vasco da Gama traced a route across the oceans to India, whose land routes were blocked by Islam. The world to be won for Christ expanded in unexpected proportions. While licking its wounds and returning to the purity of its origins, the Church dispatched its apostles to newly discovered lands. The missionary epic begins. God's people *will* spread to the ends of the earth, while an inner renewal causes them to grow in holiness.

We Must Continue to Spread the Gospel

The Gospel cries out to us today that we must not stop. "Here we have no lasting city, but we seek the city which is to come" (Heb 13:14). Our history is being faithfully written on the canvas Jesus laid out. Only the Father knows the Day and Hour when his children, having completed their earthly task, will make way for new heavens and a new earth. That will be the end, but as St. Augustine says, it will have no end.

Usually, the word "eternity" conjures up an idea of indefinite duration. This is not enough, for the eternal life reserved for us is marked even more by a change in quality. It will be an introduction to the infinite life of God, a participation in his science, his power, and his love. It will be life in all its fullness: a sublime counterpart to the incarnation of the Son of God. Jesus annihilated himself by taking on our condition. We, however, "shall be like him, for we shall see him as he is" (1 Jn 3:2). The naked immortality of the philosophers and the motionless ecstasy of the Eastern mystics will be left far behind. In Christian revelation, this static bliss is replaced by blessed life, and thus the whole joy of living. We will spend our eternity in a fruitful activity of unending interest, and the whole range of enriching fraternal relationships with other living beings.

A time will come when our earth will have completed its service. Let us leave it to God's wisdom to bring about its reconstruction and transfiguration. "No eye has seen, nor ear heard, nor the heart of man conceived, what God has prepared for those who love him" (1 Cor 2:9). Will we be among those who lament Christ's return, or among those who raise their heads? That strictly depends on us. Which road are we traveling now, the one that leads to the Lord, or the one that leads away from him? Every minute of this present life is a seed for eternity. Are our will, our spirit, and our body consecrated to God? Only then will we be among the chosen ones whom the angels will gather on the last day.

However, the elect will only receive their transformed bodies on the Last Day, once the number of the blessed has been fulfilled. This resurrection of bodies will inaugurate the future epoch. And the greater the number of the saved, the more magnificent will be God's glory and our happiness. So let's not waste a moment. Salvation is a *universal* work. Yet not all nations have been evangelized, nor has all creation received the Gospel. Perhaps there are people close to us who have not yet "found" the road that leads to Life either. Our Savior is waiting for us to show it to them.

Our primary duty as Christians is to bring as many fellow humans as we can to receive the salvation that Jesus Christ earned for all. The first disciples began spreading the Gospel without delay; the second Christian generation continued the work and passed it on to the next. And so it continues to this day. We must continue the work of our predecessors. A new page has turned in history. The Church is counting on our generosity and daring to increase the number of the blessed who will enter the life of the coming age.

20

The Return of the Master

For the Son of man is to come with his angels in the glory of his Father, and then he will repay every man for what he has done.

—Matthew 16:27

The Pharisees largely rejected the Messiah because they thought the kingdom would belong to them by right. Why did they need to convert, as if they were sinners? In the end, Jesus tells them that others will take their place in that kingdom, while they themselves will be thrown out. For Christians, as it was for the Chosen People, baptism guarantees no right to heaven. Our title of children of God will not save us, if we do not behave as children of God. That's why, at the end of his preaching, the Savior eagerly made clear the severity of his demands, and showed us how to meet them.

While the Father alone knows the day of judgement, Jesus emphasizes its suddenness. The world will not wait. It will be like in the days of Noah:

> For as in those days before the flood they were eating and drinking, marrying and giving in marriage, until the day when Noah entered the ark, and they did not know until the flood came and swept them all away, so will be the coming of the Son of man. (Mt 24:38–39)

In an intentionally apocalyptic style, Our Lord lets us know that those whose conduct seems similar will be punished differently. Not everyone who calls themselves a Christian will necessarily be admitted to heaven: One will be taken, another left behind.

"You only die once," say people who are afraid of death, to reassure themselves. That's the point: You have to get it right the first time. And to be sure of a successful death, you have to live well. On that day, luminous for the chosen, dark for the reprobate—one will be taken and the other left. "There will be two women grinding together; one will be taken and the other left" (Lk 17:35). Not only are the occupations the same, but the saved and the damned perform them *together.* There seems to be no difference between them, and yet they are suddenly separated. The Lord does not judge on the outside, for "he knew all men and needed no one to bear witness of man" (Jn 2:25). Some deceive those around them, others deceive themselves; appearances and illusions vanish under the gaze of the One who searches hearts and minds.

God Will Judge Us by Our Love

Behind the materiality of our deeds, the Lord sees the secret intention that guided us, the intimate thoughts and deep desires that imbued our actions with their true moral quality. You've done nothing wrong: That's hardly reassuring for a Christian. Have you done all the good God expected of you? Consider the excitement of the servants in the parable when they learn that the Master has returned. He turned up unexpectedly, and everyone had to account to him for the way they had handled his property. He had not entrusted everyone with an equal amount of money, but had proportioned responsibilities according to each person's ability; so the servants were not rewarded according to the gain they had made, but according to their work. One presents him with ten talents, the other with four: It doesn't matter. They have both done their best with the gifts they received, and their fate will be the same. They will share in the eternal bliss of the kingdom. But the servant who runs to withdraw his master's money from where he had hidden it, to be sure of returning it, the lazy man who, having done nothing wrong, has done nothing right, this useless servant will weep and gnash his teeth in the darkness.

The servant who buried his master's money had not misused his talent. His fault was not to use it at all. His condemnation came in two words: *worthless servant* (Mt 25:30). A servant who does not serve is no longer a servant; a Christian who does not Christianize is no longer a Christian. What good were the gifts God bestowed on him if he did not use them to extend the reign of God in and around himself? He was supposed to glorify the heavenly Father by virtuous deeds and show men the truth and beauty of the Gospel. But he didn't share his Christianity, he didn't make his communions bear fruit, he put his lamp under a bushel, he hid his treasure. Because he didn't care about the salvation of others, he compromised his own salvation.

Yet, Lord, I have believed in you, and I have not forsaken your Church. Listen to the story of several young girls who made up the bridal party at the wedding of one of their friends (see Mt 25:1–13). It may seem improbable, but the bridegroom couldn't be bothered to show up. It was pitch-dark, and everyone in the wedding party was dozing off to sleep. Suddenly, at midnight, a cry rang out: "Behold, the bridegroom! Come out to meet him" (Mt 25:6). The bridesmaids awake, preparing the lamps that will light the bridal procession. Five of the bridesmaids had taken the necessary supply of oil in a flask to feed the flame of their lamp; the other five had neglected this precaution. A fatal oversight. The bridegroom, who has made others wait, doesn't wait for them: He takes with him only those who are ready.

And so, at the hour of the great awakening, all the faithful will emerge from their tombs, but will they presume recklessly on their common faith? "What does the oil of the lamps mean," asks St. Augustine, "is it not charity?" Only those will accompany the bridegroom who have given proof of their love. The Lord will not ask me to have done great things, but to have shown him great love in the smallest things. The little duties of each day, the small sacrifices of ordinary life, the little virtues of the home are great works in his eyes, when I do them to please him.

The whole Christian law comes down to love. God is Love, and he loved mankind so much that he embraced our humanity to the point of becoming one with it. We can only love God if we love his Son, and we cannot love his Son unless we love all our brothers and sisters. It is on this summary precept of charity that the world will be judged.

How to Wait for Christ

Christians who await their Master are also always attentive to the thought of the Savior within them. They speak to him and hear him. It's as if he's already arrived.

"*Marana-tha,* come, Lord Jesus!" The Christian who awaits the Master obeys his commands; and better still, strives to foresee his desires. The faithful Christian is thoughtful. Seeing Jesus in each of their brothers and sisters, Christians become providence to those around them, the living Gospel that Christianizes the world in which they live. Christians are happy with the trouble they take to satisfy the Master, and they don't worry about tomorrow because the Master may come back *tonight*.

The Christian waits for the Master with patience. Christ's followers aren't immune to adversity, but neither does it overwhelm them. We do not curse suffering, but forgive those who afflict us, "for this slight momentary affliction is preparing for us an eternal weight of glory beyond all comparison" (2 Cor 4:17). Christians who await the return of the Master rise under the blows of bad fortune. Their energy is tempered by difficulties, and they cling to the cross on which it is possible for them to share in the redemptive atonement of Calvary.

The Christian awaits the return of his Master with clarity and joy. What kind of Christian would delay to restore order to their life until the last hour? A mercenary calculation, when God wants to be *loved*! The Christian is always ready for the hour of death. What's more, our ignorance doesn't worry us. We know that, guided by his love, he who knows the hour of our departure has chosen the best one for us. Moreover, we can thank him for not knocking on our door when perhaps we did not regret our sin.

The Master doesn't want to enter a sad and darkened house. He wants to be greeted with a shout of joy. When he left his servants, he expressly told them: "I will see you again and your hearts will rejoice, and no one will take your joy from you" (Jn 16:22). Christians who moan about their ills, or sulk about their time, or put on a victim's face—how can they teach people to love the Gospel? Their light must shine in the eyes of others to lead them to give glory to God! The Father has brought them from darkness into the kingdom of his Son—how could joy not shine from their faces!

Salvation is a free gift from God. But if we are not sure of ourselves, we can be sure of his goodness. The Christian's hope is not an irrational impulse, but a gift from God with which we strive to respond to his thoughtfulness. God loves us in the light, but we can only love him in the dark. We see only a corner of the tapestry's reverse side, but even so we can declare it a masterpiece. Such is our confidence, that understanding almost nothing of his purposes, we nevertheless proclaim that all he does is well done.

21

The Lord Comes

> It is full time now for you to wake from sleep. . . .
> Put on the Lord Jesus Christ.
>
> —Romans 13:11, 14

The cataclysm begins. While careless or unbelieving men die of fright, Christians raise their heads, hailing the hour of their deliverance. The time has come to awaken from slumber. On a new earth, the righteous will take part in the triumph of Jesus Christ, whose reign is now uncontested and definitive. He himself will hand over the kingdom to his Father.

This day of the Coming, if it rightly frightens the backward who have not rejected the works of darkness, brings immense joy to Christians who trust simply in the Lord. Christ's triumph will be the hour of our deliverance.

Let's stand up straight and lift our heads, we're going to become fully human at last. Our feeble minds try to contemplate the triumph of the "whole Christ." As St. Augustine used to say: Christ with all the members of his Body.[1] His glorious advent will be that of the eternal Church, a splendid transfiguration of the Church on earth which, in its streams of love and holiness, will have carried away so many sins and so many human weaknesses. We will no longer have to excuse or defend her; she will be all holy. Our Church will appear in its perfect beauty, in the image of the one who was its figure and model, the immaculate Virgin Mary, illuminator of the first days of Advent, gateway to heaven, through whom the Son of God came to inhabit our earth. How great is the whole body of Christ! The eternal Church gathers redeemed humanity into her bosom.

What short philosophies of history today's materialistic thinkers indulged. This was all they could invent: a herd of unfortunates destined to ensure the earthly felicity of the next generation; a well-being whose price is no less costly than the evils from which it relieves us; a few glimmers of a happiness barely tasted in the midst of suffering; hatred and wars; and all this only to sink into nothingness! They declared creation absurd, seemingly unaware that the absurdity lay in detaching creation from its Creator.

---

1. See *Catechism of the Catholic Church* no. 1364, and "Homily 21" in Augustine's *Homilies on the Gospel of John*, ed. Boniface Ramsey (New City Press, 2009), nos. 377–380.

When the Lord returns in his glory, we'll be able to read with a single glance the marvelous history of mankind, its moral ascents cut short by dreadful relapses. We'll contemplate the history of God's people from whom the Savior of the world was to be born. And we will see the ferment of Christians gradually lifting the inert mass, the slow progress of the Gospel raising all peoples to Christ, to make them forever sons of God.

How we shall acclaim our Christ on the day of his victory! What thanksgiving we will give him! With the angels, we'll prostrate ourselves before the Holy Trinity and sing his glory.

The First Signs

Until Christ comes again, his reign will expand over the earth. The outpouring of the Holy Spirit on his Church, the ruin of Judaism, and the preaching of the Gospel to the Gentiles will be its immediate manifestations. Jesus announced it: The generation listening to him would not disappear before seeing these first signs of his kingdom (Mk 9:1); they would occur before the apostles had time to evangelize all the cities of Israel (Mt 10:23). The progress of the kingdom of God continues from the time of the Incarnation to that of the Parousia.

The Church's liturgy continually places us before this immense fresco of Redemption, regularly directing our gaze toward the glorious phase of the advent of the new Adam, drawing redeemed humanity into his victory. It is often tempting to see the liturgical year merely as a reminder and representation of past events, and as a kind of teaching through action of the Christian faith. This undoubtedly defines the liturgical year, but only as a secondary aspect, and one that shouldn't be overemphasized. The liturgical season and feasts are not a historical re-enactment comparable to the medieval dramas of the Nativity and the Passion. Such a revival of the past would be artificial and practically impossible. When, during Advent, we hear the prophet's moving calls to the Savior who is to come, let us beware of believing that we must fictitiously replicate the attitudes of the righteous who sighed for the coming of the Messiah. For us, he has already come, and he has already accomplished the redemptive sacrifice.

If the liturgy instructs us, and it does, its main purpose is not didactic. "As often as the sacrifice of the Cross by which 'Christ our Pasch has been sacrificed' is celebrated on the altar, the work of our redemption is carried out."[2] The work of our redemption is taking

---

2. *Catechism of the Catholic Church*, no. 1364.

place now, and will continue until the Final Coming. The Christ of the liturgy is not the Christ of the past, but the "whole Christ," with all his members from age to age. Everything happens today. At Christmas, it's today that we're born into divine life; in the Passion, it's today that we die to sin. It's today that the Ascension ushers us into the heavens. It's still today that the Son of God redeems the world.

When we commemorate the great dates of our redemption, Christ takes shape in us and models us in his image, so that we may resemble him on the Day of the Meeting. But his reign grows in us only if we make it grow in the world, to multiply the chosen ones for the day of his triumph. This is what the annual solemnities invite us to do each year. The peace offered to people of good will on Christmas night, the light of Epiphany that enlightens the pagans, the cross that has spread joy throughout the world, "the Spirit that renews the face of the earth," all remind us of the missionary task of those whom Christ "sends as the Father sent him" (see John 20:21), "not wishing that any should perish, but that all should reach repentance" (2 Pt 3:9).